the
letter
ji

THE LETTER JI

© 2013 by Ji Hyun Jung

Published in Grand Rapids, Michigan, by The Letter Ji.

ISBN-13: 978-0-615-85448-9

Cover design: Ji H. Jung
Cover photography: Ji H. Jung
Interior design: Ji H. Jung

Printed in the United States of America
First Edition 2013

God, You show me over and over again
that You do, indeed, make beautiful things
out of the broken and incomplete.

To everyone holding on.

Contents

Hi. My name is Ji.
Yeah, like the letter.
(G)

I need you to read this part aloud.
I don't care if you're in a bookstore,
by your friends,
by strangers,
or by yourself.

C'mon, at least whisper it
under your breath, okay?:

"I matter.
I am stunning.
I have potential.
I don't look stupid doing this.
I'm not alone."

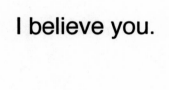

Foreword

by Tate Kirgiss

It's kind of a funny story. I met Ji right around the time I was turning twenty-one. We were both at a Young Life camp up in northern Michigan. We spent a summer working together along with a handful of other college students. This was the first time I encountered Ji in person—the laugh, the sass, the whole package. But this was not the first time she began to impact my life.

Let me take you back a few months prior to the June of the same year. Ji was a complete stranger to me. I had no idea of her existence. But her name happened to catch my eye on the list of the people I would be serving with come summer. I was undergoing a time of struggle in my life during this season and only God knows why...but I decided to reach out to her for help. You must understand, I am not the kind of person to be openly transparent about the hardships I face in life. And maybe that is why I reached out to Ji—she was an absolute clean slate. She knew nothing of who I was. She knew nothing of my past or the places I had been. Ji had no preconceived judgments about my character or personality. With a relatively awkward hello and a beginning to what soon became an outpour of my heart via text and e-mails, something radical happened. Little did I know I was coming in contact with my soon-to-be best friend. Ji responded with an abundance of love, affirmation, and direction. She took a broken heart of someone she had never met and gave an honest amount of time to care.

You see, that's who Ji is.

Ji cares.

Ji loves.

Ji lifts up.

There is no specific agenda with her.

She is simply with you.

And after a while, I have come to realize that she does it because she has been cared for, loved, and lifted up by her heavenly Father. This is evident after meeting her for five minutes. I promise. Ji's heart is ten times too big for her to keep in her body—so she doesn't. And you can't stop her either. She shares it freely with everyone she comes into contact with. If I recall correctly, this is also why Ji decided to write this book. She needed to share something...something huge.

This girl has been my best friend since we met. No—not the kind of "best friend" who sees every new movie that comes out with you and is in all of your spring break photos. (Although it does frequently happen.) Ji Hyun Jung is the *best* kind of best friend. She is the one who reminds me of my worth, affirms me in my silly adventures to be a musician, checks in on me at just the right time, and *always* reminds me that it's all about Jesus. Always.

If you have already met Ji, you should know well why you ought to read this book. But if you haven't, let me tell you— as someone whose life has been drastically changed for the better because of her story intertwining with mine—this book will leave a positive mark in your life. It is a real story about a real girl who found her real Savior, and she wants the world to know who He is.

I introduce you to Ji. Enjoy.

—Tate Kirgiss
songwriter and worship leader at Campus House

You can check out Tate's music at: www.tatekirgiss.com

Preface

For all you know, I am as short and precise as Helvetica and according to your keen observations thus far, I'm Asian. Who am I, really, for you to take the words I write to heart? Let's just get some things out of the way so we are at a more intimate level than a standard reader-writer relationship:

My favorite color is green.

If I were to be an animal, I am a sea otter. (This is different than what animal I aspire to be though. I wish I could be a lioness. My hope is that I can be like a lioness one day.)

I like mangoes.

I like peach rings, too.

I prefer odd numbers over even.

I still casually pick my nose from time to time.

And I think we just became closer friends.

***

When I first began to work on this book, my friends kept asking me what I was writing about. Some were questioning out of mere curiosity while others were transparently saying, "What on earth are you an expert on that you all of a sudden have this need to enlighten the world?"

It was a fair question. And to be frank, I didn't know how to answer it right. If I am not mistaken, I have spewed out a different response every time. They were all along the same lines, but what I was writing about was something beyond what I could fit in a 140-character content.

You see, I have always wanted to write a book. But it was never for the right reasons. Then came Christmas break of last year. I was back in my hometown and I was walking in a familiar place amongst unfamiliar faces and something about the situation tugged on my physical heart to a degree where I needed to stop what I was doing.

I had no idea where any of these people were from or where they were headed but I wholeheartedly wondered if they knew how precious their lives were.

I watched a little girl gaze at the wonder of some celebrity I do not know on the front page of a magazine with eyes that screamed envy and self-doubt. I breathed in every strut that spoke boredom and apathy around me; it made me nauseous. A mother to my left was so engaged at the options of hair products that the fact that her son's pacifier dropped to the ground was a complete mystery, and I was still standing there wondering why I was not doing anything about it.

Call me weird, but I began to wonder if we would be carrying ourselves in this seemingly exhausted manner if we truly did not know tomorrow was in guaranteed reach. From all of the conversations unheard to the potential lives that could not only change, but be saved.

I wanted to share something I have that keeps me from being bored, I guess. There is something important happening right now and it seriously kills me inside to know that *anyone* could be missing it. I do not know much, but I do know one thing: Jesus saved my life. I am no doctor. I am no pastor. Nor am I good at this by any means. I just know what I have seen and I know what keeps me from fearing death. I also know why I live for the moment.

Because death is a lie.

***

You'll learn quickly that I am a believer of miracles. No—not like the "I went to Disney World and it was a dream" kind of miracles, I am talking about serious miracles that have become so seemingly obsolete in this world. I don't take it for granted that you've picked up this book. There could quite possibly be something has been embedded in here that you might just take to heart. I hope that we can have fun, grow a bit here and there, maybe laugh, perhaps even cry, definitely feel something, and ultimately move forward with this life with an extra skip in our step because hope is on our side.

Introduction

I t starts out on a gravel road. The overall vision is in sepia but perhaps it is simply because my culturally engaged brain is recalling this from 1994. My little hand engulfed within his, we are walking home. I am not sure where we are coming from but I am pretty sure I know where we are going. I also cannot not tell you how long it takes or what route we decide on because I have grape gummies in my hand.

Man, am I excited to open up this package. This is literally all my three-year-old self can handle right now. But I look across the room. I guess somewhere between here and there, we are now here, inside. But indeed I look across and there stand my mother and father. Seems important. Also seems boring. I would much rather concentrate on getting the grape gummies inside my mouth, please.

It is a struggle. I need help. I look across again but I am too little for them to see my struggle. They are all the way on the other side of a room; my struggle is not even present right now. It is okay. I wait. Until then, I stare at the purple, round, tasty little morsels that are so close to my taste buds and yet so far away. I entertain thoughts. I make funny noises. Squish a few of them with my fingers as I trace the outline of the one I will consume first. I imagine everything about them.

I forget, this dream can still happen; bigger people are around with bigger hands and bigger knowledge to open my now desperately wrinkled package. So I take my eyes away from the grape gummies once more to see something different.

Noises.

There is a lot of it. There is so much noise that I cannot hear anything, actually. In my world, it is dead silent that you can only hear a pin drop. They start circling each other— mother and father, I mean. Like the hyenas in *The Lion King*, faces become weird and sharp and I do not like it.

Why am I still here?

I do not think I want to be here. Nope. There is too much noise and I cannot understand anything no one is helping me I want my grape gummies and I see sharp faces and sharp movements and there are probably sharp words but I do not know much I just want to focus on what is truly important here and it feels like it is the gummies.

Mother is thrown to the ground.

I hear a pin drop inside me. Noise breaks loose again. But no one is actually making any sound this time.

I am unreasonably calm and collected, probably because my mind is elsewhere. Probably because I am still tracing the first gummy I will eat with my index finger. But even little persons know when something is not right.

I crawl toward her face.

"Where is mom? Where did she go? Why is she not here?"

I play with her limp lips like a puppeteer.

"Mom. Mama. Talk to me. Helloooooo."

Confused.

I am so confused right now. I look across the room and now father is where I once stood. He is never really near. I do not see his face. I can only see his knees and his ankles. His black socks.

He says, "Ji, no. It's okay. It's alright. Mama *and* papa are here. Look. Come to me!"

I open my mouth to respond to the socks, "No. You are not."

***

To this day I am not sure why I chose grape gummies. I used to say it was my least favorite flavor. This is my earliest memory. And so it begins.

Chapter One:

The Uncontrollables

I was born in Pusan, South Korea, where the rich and poor collide but never meet. When I was three, my father became a raging alcoholic due to stress and failed expectations. There is not much I remember other than a few broken chairs and burnt pictures. When I was four, my mother filed for divorce because of different stress and different kinds of failed expectations. She picked up a full-time job as a travel agent to escape her world and most of my memories with her were the ones when she would wake me up only to kiss me goodbye. When I was five, I started to make my own meals and walk myself home from school. And when I was six, I learned that certain people can play children all their lives and people like me were robbed of the idea.

As much as I wanted to, I never ran away. I didn't reject this lifestyle. In fact, I caved inward and spiraled toward the pursuit of denial and perfection. I searched for rectification instead. Half of it was simply being too naïve of my very real circumstances and the other half was that I constantly felt this need to one day prove to the world that I made it through without messing it up completely.

***

A few months ago, I had the opportunity to take a small road trip with my dear friend Jane. I enjoy road trips because there is no escape to it. Not really. Once you're into it, you're stuck, at least for a little while. The people. The destination. The conversations. And the two hundred potty breaks in between. You must be present for it all. I enjoy road trips because it forces you to see the real you amongst other people being their real selves.

Jane has short, idyllic hair and the cutest button-nose you'd ever seen. I'm serious. She embraces everyone she meets with warmth that can only be described by the sun and she does not take bullcrap for an answer. She is also the same age as my mother. And a few things I have gathered within my mere twenty-one years of life regarding folks my mother's age is that they are beautifully blunt.

Within about fifteen minutes on the road, Jane asked me to tell her my life story. The drone of the air conditioning set a nice medium and her silent GPS told me we had a long ways to go. We had known one another for a decent while at that point and it did seem rather silly that we hardly knew each other's pasts.

My *life story*, though?

How did one really tell his or her life story in one sitting?

I felt like every time I had been asked to talk about the places I had been and the person that I used to be, I had told it differently. I also felt as though I had failed as a storyteller every time. (So this is kind of comedic that I am writing this book as we speak.)

"It's a complicated story," I began to say.

Jane turned down the radio by several big notches and took a generous sip from her coffee mug, "That's completely fine. We're not in a rush to get anywhere."

I took a quick glance at Jane just in the nick of time to catch her smirking at me. It was true. We weren't in a rush at all. It was just me and Jane on an open road with open ears and open hearts.

***

You do not see mold growing until one day it is there and you ask yourself *how* and *when.* Like all things we that do not care to pay attention to, it will still develop if it is not properly taken care of. Weeds will continue to grow unless you pull from the roots. Stains will become harder to get rid of as you wait to dissolve the content completely. Wars continue to rage in places we do not know, and gossip will keep spreading unless you personally stomp it out with confrontation. And like all else in this book, I am going to talk about the heart.

Walls are built up around our hearts where damage has been done, much like scabs attempting to heal the wound. Except with these walls, they do not necessarily protect the heart; they rather numb it. We mistake this numbing sensation to be safety when it is working much like a drug. Our souls cling to feel nothing and the moment this fails, we work to build another wall. When one does not carefully observe this in its progress, he or she will eventually forget what the shape of his or her heart initially looked like because the layers of walls are absolutely remarkable.

I would know this process well.

I was the most diligent of this kind of architecture.

***

As I began to unveil the details in the fabric of my life, Jane quietly paid attention as though she was listening to classical music. Her expression was soft and she received every sentence like she was collecting the pieces for a later time.

In my head, it wasn't classical music that was being composed for exhibition but rather an impromptu pop song with sporadic choruses about my left shoe and a tiger. The little workers in my brain were moving about frantically to reconstruct the memories about my past as my mouth did its best to relay the information to Jane's ears. This was because the last time I had really told my story was prior to last Christmas. And during last Christmas, Jesus showed up. He changed everything I had ever known about the truths about my life because He invaded my heart that night. He tore down walls like a tsunami. These walls around my heart used to own me. These walls that I had invested years in their making were once the backboard of how I responded to everything in this world. In the passing of one winter's night, they were gone.

***

As Jane offered me this opportunity to reflect, I realized something truly monumental. Since last Christmas, I had not thought about my past. This was bizarre for me because the past used to be the size of a mountain in the landscape of my mind and I dwelled on it frequently. I had no idea what my perspective of my past looked like anymore as I tried to share my life events. Quite frankly, it was because my heart was no longer attached. Little did Jane know that she was not the only one in the car hearing this newly found story for the first time.

***

When I was almost seven, I went to a restaurant with my mom. It was high up in a building somewhere. The halls were colorful but the air was dim and brittle. Everything about the experience was unfamiliar. The music, the fancy napkins, and the way my rubber flip-flops felt on the marble floor...but mostly the man. He was the most unfamiliar. My mother took me on a date with someone who I was to call 'dad' in less than a month and I was sold on this deal because he bought me a yellow balloon that night. In the same year, there was a wedding, a honeymoon, and three plane tickets purchased en route to the United States of America.

When you're that young, you don't question motives. And when you are raised in a South Korean household, you especially don't question your parents' motives. It was not until I hit my twenties that my mother shared what this was all about.

Divorce was extremely uncommon in the culture of our country and no kid from a broken background made it far in life without some special bargain. My biological father came from an elite family and she married him at the age when he seemed to fit like a glove. Personalities rubbed and physical beauty began to fade. A wake up call rang when my father began drinking away to feel something and used my mother's paychecks to grab the taxis back home every night. Ashamed and distraught, she remarried on a whim to activate a brighter future for the both of us.

I can still recall the image as clear as day. Mother packed two duffle bags; one filled with articles of our clothing and another with a film camera and books for me to read. We stepped onto an airplane and as we landed in a far away land, we were welcomed by a one-bedroom apartment with new man to call family. It wasn't long until she was hit with the insensitive truth that immigrants also don't make it far in life without some special bargain and that love does not stem from a yellow balloon. A brighter future wasn't on the opposite end of the world. It was on the opposite end of her pride.

***

I think I always believed in God, or maybe the concept that us humans could not have been just left here on earth to run about like chickens. I think I hoped for God to be a real thing because the idea of pointlessness absolutely killed me. This was because I thought I had it hard. My world was all too consumed with this impression that I was not being pitied enough and perhaps my reward would be uncovered at the end of this tragedy. I didn't find life to be a playground and if I was suffering just because I had been placed here by coincidence, I saw it rather peculiar that I would do much to move forth.

There are certain things in life we can never entirely have control over. Much of my generation despises this reality. In fact, we dislike it so much that we are in absolute denial about it. We get plastic surgery to pretend we never needed change. We vacation to warm climates to ignore the fact that someone is still dealing with winter. We buy nice things for people to become magnetized when it was never us controlling our amiability; it was always the glamour and glitz. And we masquerade around with these smiles plastered on our faces because we inevitably live in this world and so we might as well like it. But there was once a point when I thought I could control this decision of living as well. There was a moment in my past when I didn't want to move forth with this story and the idea of cutting it short settled well with my numb heart.

As I continued sharing my history with Jane, I projected back to the evening when I scheduled to take my own life. It was a strange and uncanny feeling to recall because I was so detached and yet I, Ji, was still the character playing out the story.

I was seventeen and a popular girl with an eating disorder. I hid my good grades to pretend I was carefree and I drove extra blocks on the way home from classes everyday to avoid what was waiting for me at home. I strove for the approval from my parents that I never seemed to receive. I also heavily feared the attention that I did receive from boys. I found my relationships with my surroundings to be vain because they were built on what was visible from my appearance, which was hardly anything. The friends of mine were ever distant and the real me was absolutely unknown. Depressed. Lonely. Confused. I despised who I was on the outside and I despised who I was on the inside even more.

Also, when you are seventeen, everything is dramatic. Even ones who claim they aren't dramatic; they are oddly dramatic about it. It's just the way it is. It is an age where we think we have discovered all that there is to it and if it really is all that there is, there is no way we cannot explode in drama about it.

It was the night before a school dance. The pavements were dry with bitter gusts of wind constantly sweeping away any hint of life on the streets. I was crowned to be our area's homecoming queen at the football game no less than three hours prior and I still had silver confetti stuck in my hair because I spent most of the night driving in my beaten and tired Volkswagen Beetle, hoping to get lost. My lips were cold in the shade of fading red and I had peaked my potential of faking perfection to the world. I was about to step into the shower but before I did, I remember taking a good look into the mirror. I was thin. But my mind wasn't sure. I looked at my forehead, my mouth, my shoulders, and my hands—the hands that possessed so much power over what the next hour would've looked like.

I eyed the crown sitting unbearably stiff on my head.

The synthetic jewels of the toy were dangling so wearily by threads. I could feel its complete and utter desperateness.

What a mockery I had become. This wasn't me. Running away from the truth was the ugliest thing I saw in my mother. This was also the thing I had once promised myself never to do. Hiding and dodging to pave an easy way through life was for the weak and broken. Yet there I was, hiding, dodging, cold, and very much broken. I was as fake as the crown crushing my pride on my head.

What did it mean to be real anyway?

I was my own worst enemy. What a fool we all were to think she who receives the crown is the happiest of them all.

I looked into my eyes.

I didn't know who I was.

I didn't know whose I was.

I didn't know what I was doing here.

Identity.

My world was spinning but my days melted into one. I was living within a very fixed calendar where the concept of tomorrow was never within reach. It didn't matter if nights turned into days; I never slept anyway. I was living in constant darkness. My mind would race with thoughts about a different life, perhaps even a life I could upholster from the one at hand, but the strong and persistent current of apathy would wash these thoughts away as though hope was never written in the sand. There was no trace of it. For all I knew, it never existed. Hope was just a figment of my childlike imagination.

***

I had always kept my choice of poison inside an old guitar case cornered in my closet. Brushing it off, I found myself standing naked in front of the mirror again. My reflection was screaming at me to do something. What a shame to know I had breaths to take while people all around were counting their last. What a spoiled child I had become to not be grateful for this gift of life I had received. I remember being so puzzled. I remember staring up at the ceiling, muttering to God, *I never asked for this gift. I don't deserve it. Why did you leave me here? Why won't you take me back? You don't hear me, do you? You're not listening at all.*

The amount of selfishness I felt overwhelmed my soul. The amount of control I wanted to escape this world killed my spirit. In front of the mirror, I watched myself overdose that night. Stripped naked and transparent. I recall the shower continuously shedding hot water for an empty tub while I lay limp next to it, feeling the steam wipe away my tears.

There was also a phone call that night. It occurred seconds after I swallowed the pills. It was from my best friend at the time. She left a voicemail and it came through my phone:

Hey... Missed you tonight after the game. It wasn't the same without your face to brighten up the party. I know this might be random, but could I spend the night at your place after the dance tomorrow? My parents are fighting again and I don't really know who else to talk to about it. Thanks, Ji. I don't know what I would do without you. See you soon. Call me back as soon as you can.

As her simple, seemingly innocuous words pierced through the thick steam and shot into my seventeen-year-old heart, I heard a faint voice inside me speak softly,

You are not alone.

In an instant, I stuck my left index finger down my throat and vomited out the death that was inside of me. As I gasped for air and fell to my knees, clarity came and wrapped me intensely.

My suicide attempt wasn't a cry for help.

It was a desperate cry for attention.

It wasn't that I wanted to die.

It was that I desperately needed a Savior.

***

One word. One person. One conversation.

All it takes is one movement to alter another. It's how instants work. In an instant, there was a moment that was beyond my reach. What a brilliant and tragic thing it is that a message as meek as this could cause my heart from dying to living. To know we are wanted, needed, missed, and personally identified as an individual with our own story to tell. Most of our lives are gone by without giving recognition to the truly remarkable happenings that surround us. This seems to be because we are trapped with the lie that no one cares. What if someone were to tell us that they did care? What if it were true that none of these things were thoughtless circumstances but rather series of miracles waiting to unfold? Would we want to cut it short then, these miracles that are just about to happen, even if we had the option to?

Instants. Moments. I believe we do not give the seconds of our lives enough credit for the power and impact they hold. We rely on the years and the decades, when in reality, they would be nothing without our instants and our moments.

These single breaths that alter one eternal happening to another.

***

We don't forget about moments like this because for once in our lives, we really do believe to have all of the control. At this point in my life, I had lost control of all else; I clung to what I believed I could maintain. My physique. My reputation. My span of life. But this is a clever thing that the devil does when we allow his tricks to play with our soul. In moments like this, we have the *least* control.

I had no idea where I was headed or why I was doing anything. When we go about decisions without a clear reason or purpose, we are not in control. This is a mistake set in our mind. We might be sitting in the driver's seat for a moment, sure. But both of our hands are off the wheel and we are bound to crash.

My reasons were indefinite and obviously uncertain. But they were real. They were the realest things in my life at the time. This foggy haze of my reasons was what I woke up to every morning and breathed in before I closed my eyes to sleep. They consumed every waking hour but I did not know them well to know where to dig up the roots.

I did not know how badly I wanted control, even the parts that were left up to God. When in the midst of things, I simply thought that I was the victim the entire time when in reality, I was shaking my fist at God with disapproval of the fact that I did not reign over my own life. I wanted to escape a world where I was born into reality, as much my mother tried to escape on the plane from the concept of divorce and brokenness at home. I tried so hard to roll my own dice and to play my own cards. And the ultimate way to stick it to the man was to manually flip the switch off so that I could say I had the last word.

But thank God He knows me better than I know myself. Thank God He makes all things new. Thank God for moments. Thank God I do not know how this story is supposed to end. And thank God that I am not the one in control, for I would be shamefully frail, shamefully weak, uninspired by the world, and drifting aimlessly where there are no happy accidents or surprises. I might not even be writing this book.

***

The truth is, my thirst for control over my own life came from the wonder of where to place the blame for all of the bad things...all of the pain, all of the trials. Was it my parents? Culture? Money? Marriage? Divorce? Alcohol? Stress? Perfection? Me? This was the conclusion that drew me to despise myself. Little did I know that there was a bigger picture to be drawn. Little did I know we are in the middle of warfare between the devil and God Himself. It wasn't about me or the mistakes I had made. It was about the reality that we live in a broken world.

Maybe life wasn't given to the ones who have most control. Maybe it was truly rewarded to the ones willing to give it up. And perhaps these stories we tell are not based on how we found ourselves here, but rather how we reacted to it.

***

I believe that God was always watching over me. Like the way a shepherd observes and takes care of his sheep. Although most of my youth was spent wandering aimlessly, I believe He was guiding me the entire time with the people on the streets, or the random voicemails about just another night. Perhaps none of these things were accidents. Perhaps we are all too nearsighted to understand the mystery. I believe that there is something greater than us orchestrating all of what is happening here. There are still moments where I question why an all-knowing God would not inhibit me from looming into the dark and dangerous alleys of living. I suppose He could keep us all on a tight leash so that we are guaranteed not to fall. But then again, that would not be a trusting relationship. That would not be love. The story would end right here.

***

When Jane and I reached our destination, she looked at me and smiled. It was about four in the afternoon and the golden rays of the sun were beaming boldly into the car.

"You know, Ji, Jesus was all over that story."

"Yeah, I 'spose so," I reservedly responded, "You can never seem too sure of it at the time I guess."

"You have to be sure though, Ji. You have to give Him credit for all that He has done in the in-betweens. Because He's not the guy who just shows up one day; He's there all along."

Jane was right. She was absolutely right.

***

I suppose this is the unfolding. Here are the moments and instants before that Christmas night and the ones thereafter. This is me tracing back and giving Him credit for all of the times where I wasn't certain and He yet was certain of me.

Chapter Two:
Balloons and Hot Dogs

I did not grow up in a Christian household. I am still not quite sure what people mean when they say that. Being "Christian" is such an array of things these days, I feel. I grew up in a somewhat agnostic household up until I was nine. I remember churches rising up left and right during the few years when I did live in South Korea but my mother and I never transitioned with the movement. I also believe we were Buddhist for a day or two when we were touring around the old temples once. But something tells me that hardly counts. We simply lived, for the most part. We didn't question much and there never seemed to be a significant point to do so.

Like I have mentioned before, the immigrant life wasn't (and still isn't) an easy one. Other than my mother's high-strung hope for providing me with the most optimal life option, we also moved to the United States for the sake of my stepfather's employment. The term "employment" is very vague in this sense. He wasn't employed, necessarily. Rather, he was an aspiring entrepreneur like many of the other immigrants trying to make something of themselves when moving to this free land of America where dreams can happen and discrimination isn't real. My mother put all of her eggs in this basket and it has been quite a ride, to say the least.

My stepfather leased a small piece of property in the heart of downtown Grand Rapids, Michigan, and started up a dry cleaning business. The little bit of my mother's money that had not yet been stolen and abused by my biological father went into this sanctuary of hope. Why dry cleaning? Because Asians have a knack for being absurdly meticulous about cleanliness and precision. That, and there never needed to be much verbal explanation when communicating to someone that one's clothing is either dirty or too small for his or her waistline. It was manageable for my newly dubbed parents and it was paid work. And any work at that point was valuable.

The two would courageously get up at the crack of dawn every morning and clean up the vacant lot to make it worth something while our apartment was nothing much to call a home either. I remember this season in our lives well because I had to tag along for all of its bumps and bruises. Our grand opening banner hung low and the open sign was made of lined paper and pen. I was only seven at the time but even I knew that this was pitiful.

My mother would make me bring a sketchbook and a pencil with them on the weekends so that I could practice my multiplication tables while I'd watch her anxiously wait for a customer to walk through those rusty, unwelcoming doors. Every time she caught me drawing pictures in the pages instead of my math, she would hit my wrists and call me ungrateful. I hated going to work with them but they said I was too young to stay at the apartment by myself. I wasn't fond of staying back either but at least then I didn't have to study my multiplication tables all the time.

"Mom, why do I have to work on these?" I would ask on a regular basis in my respectful yet peeved voice. I went through roughly twenty pages per day and even that never seemed to be satisfactory.

"So that you can make something of yourself, Ji-Hyun! So that you can become rich with the knowledge in your head and the dignity in your heart!" Mother would respond while pointing at my head and my chest as though I wouldn't know otherwise.

"But what if I don't want to be rich?"

Mother despised it when I talked back.

"Don't be absurd, Ji-Hyun," she'd say, "Do you want to grow up like me? To work in a place like this and to live in a home like that? Do you want to labor at other people's feet when you are older? No. You have potential. Don't you dare flush that down the toilet. You're going to become a heroic leader. You're going to change the world. And all leaders know their multiplication tables. You will thank me later. You will live a life I never could."

I would walk away murmuring the multiples of five, glancing back to see my mother with a glistening tear rolling down her thin cheek. This conversation happened more frequent than it should have and if I had collected all of the tears from my mother's eyes, I would have had enough to fill an ocean.

When I was turning eight, Jung-Min was born. To this day, she is one of the greatest mercies of my life. To call her my half-sister is an understatement. Ever since I could remember, she was wholly my sister. She was the only family I knew well. She was the only family I felt comfortable with. She never talked much because of being a baby and such. And maybe this is why I confided in her; we both were kept quiet without much of a choice and she was there to experience it all with me. She reminded me that I was not alone.

In the tiny hospital room, there was a lot of noise but not a lot of people. I remember looking around and feeling as though the atmosphere was incomplete. I wished there were balloons. My baby sister was born; it should have been a celebration. I also wished there were more friends. But it was just me, my stepfather, my mother and Jung-Min. As the documents were getting signed, I whispered to my mother that our newborn family member should go by an American name instead. Both of my parents looked at me disappointed, almost as though I was insulting our culture and heritage. But from the single year I had lived in the United States thus far, I knew the difficulty of having a foreign name.

I told my parents that Jasmin was a pretty name. Perhaps we could legally give her a South Korean name but refer to her with an American one. It sounded similar to their original choice and somehow by the grace of God, they agreed.

***

When my mother was released from the hospital, it wasn't long until she felt the urge to go back to work. There was still a lot to be done and it would have taken a miracle to feed all four of our mouths without both parents working. The truth is, there was always a lot needed to be done. The more honest truth was that we didn't know how to slow down. Life was but a constant swirl of pandemonium amongst a bigger swirl of disorder and we were always reaching, never achieving.

But one time we reached without knowing.

And it touched something good.

In the same year of Jasmin's birth, our family was introduced to the Choi family. Somehow through the grapevine and mutual connections, we met this South

Korean family and, in retrospect, it indeed was a miracle in disguise. But like many things with God, little did we know that it was such a gift from Him at the time as much as we found it to be simply coincidence. Along with assisting my parents with business tips and becoming a close family friend to help take care of Jasmin, they also had two daughters, one of them being very close to my age.

Her name was Grace.

Grace quickly changed the way I saw everything in my life.

***

I was allowed to spend many nights over at Grace's house and I remember this being a big deal. In the past, my mother usually preferred having me stay in my room to read and study rather than going out and playing on a regular basis. But with a newborn in the picture along with many odd ends to take care of, it was rather relieving to have an eight-year-old out of the house every now and then.

When I would go over to Grace's, we'd do things I had never tried before. I was introduced to sledding for the first time. I also ate my first hot dog. It wasn't the best food, nor was sledding the most ideal thing to do in jeans, but all of it was better than anything I had known in the past. We were allowed to be messy and we were allowed to be nonsense. But the thing I found most peculiar was when we would all gather together for dinner every night. Grace's father would come home just in time for her mother to finish cooking and we would sit around their table to hold hands and pray.

I had never prayed before I met Grace.

I didn't know what we were doing, nor did I understand why Grace's father would never miss a dinner together, but I liked it.

I liked it a lot.

***

A year had passed since meeting the Choi's and Jasmin was now crawling and saying syllables of all sorts. It was late-May and everything was becoming sticky. Things were more chaotic than ever regarding the situation at my parent's work and I was still trying to grasp the concept of third grade. It was a school night when the following conversation occurred and I remember it as though it was yesterday. It is particularly memorable because all four of us happened to be home for dinner. You must understand. In our household, this was very unlikely. My stepfather would usually return home around one in the morning because we did not have it in the budget to hire others at the dry cleaner and my mother would make it home just a few minutes prior only for the sake of nursing Jasmin. The two would get about four hours of sleep every night while I did as well due to fear of sleeping by myself in an empty apartment.

As my mother and stepfather gathered around the dinner table and began to eat their food, I quietly sat there and hesitated to touch my chopsticks.

"Well, you are going to eat, aren't you?" my mother said.

I kept sitting there as the old rotating fan was messing up my hair in intervals of seven seconds.

"Maybe she's on a diet," my stepfather chuckled.

He hardly laughed but when he did, it never seemed to be the type of humor I understood. His voice was raspier than ever due to his two packs of cigarettes he began to average per day and the scent of old smoke pushed on my throat like a concrete wall.

I waited for one more round of the fan to blow a gust of wind toward the back of my neck and then I asked,

"Why don't we pray?"

Silence.

My stepfather was quick to take another spoonful of rice into his mouth. He glanced over at my mother as though she ought to reply before he did.

"I'm just wondering. Why don't we pray?" I said again.

My mother stood up to get something to drink from the fridge and moved with an awkward amount of haste,

"Ji-Hyun, what kind of a question is that? What do you mean?"

My mother wouldn't look at me in the eyes, nor would she stop moving.

I didn't know how else to ask it. So I failed to rephrase,

"I mean, why don't we pray?"

I had never seen my mother lacking words to say before. I'd usually have to meticulously peep in between her rapid speech. But this time, there was so much silence that we were all drowning in it. The fan kept rotating and all of our hairs were tousling about like helpless fish in the sea.

A minute later, she finally spoke, "We do pray, Ji-Hyun. We just do it on the inside. Some people close their eyes and stuff, right? Well, we don't have time for that. We just do it in our hearts and move on. No need to make a scene, you know? Anyway, does anyone else want anything to drink?"

"But Grace's family closes their eyes. They also hold hands."

"Well we aren't Grace's family."

"Do we believe in God?"

More silence.

***

I remember being sent to my room that night. It wasn't really a form of punishment as much as it was an excuse to end our uncomfortable dinner conversation. The one time we were all together for dinner, I made it weird and reminded everyone why we didn't do it too often. Mother had even forgotten to tell me to read or study. But my questions did not stop in my head and they boggled around like fireflies trapped inside of a jar.

A few weeks later, I asked my parents if I could carpool to church with Grace's family. Looking back, this was oddly brave. I was not an outspoken girl, nor did I usually know what I wanted. But I was curious about what Grace's family did. I began attending church when I was nine and this was when our lives really began to stir.

***

I don't really know what I expected church to be. But if anything, I guess I wanted us to go sledding in jeans more and meet other people who would embrace nonsense. I thought perhaps someone would introduce me to the guy Grace's family always seemed to be praying to and then maybe I could tell my parents about him, too. Maybe then somehow we would become nicer people with each other and everything would be easier. Maybe then I wouldn't have to do my multiplication tables all the time and my parents wouldn't be stressed out as much. It just seemed like it would work out that way. But instead, I found myself more confused than ever.

***

I remember the first lesson I walked into as a churchgoer. The message was about a boat and how a special man found two of every kind of animal to fit into this boat. We colored pictures from this particular story and a kid named Sean kept stealing my brown crayon.

As I tried connecting the dots from this animal-loving man to Grace's family holding hands at dinnertime, I began to think that church was nothing more than a building built for people to fake niceness with one another and to tell make-believe stories to pass time. I didn't seem to be learning the concept of how to get my parents to eat dinner with me every night and this whole concept of prayer was something no one seemed to really explain. It didn't kill my curiosity as much as it killed my spirit.

Another time I went to church, I was handed a Bible to share with the kids sitting next to me during the service. It was the first time in my life holding a Bible. We were supposed to find a specific passage to read along with the speaker but I had no idea how to do such a task. Instead, I flipped to a random page and pretended to follow along while I secretly read the words that were on the pages before me. Amusingly, it talked about the consequences of sin. It was surrounded by many words I did not know but I did recognize *destruction* and *death*. I also remember being scared out of my mind.

I didn't know who to ask about it. I hardly knew the people at the church and most would walk around with judgment in their eyes. I thought maybe they looked at me this way because I didn't come with my own set of parents or perhaps it was because I didn't wear lovely clothes like they did. These were the reasons I would receive these kinds of looks when I was on the streets in South Korea. But as far as why I was getting them at church, I wasn't quite sure. But I was confident I needed to keep going to church anyway because something about destruction and death might happen to me if I didn't.

***

The thing about God is that He never gives up on us. Even when we don't get it and we throw our hands up along with the white flag, He remains. Not only that, but He remains relentless. Sometimes I wish it wasn't so true because He can be downright incessant sometimes. But I have come to realize that the moments when I become most irritated with God is when I need Him the most. He never seems to allow me to let go, not completely.

***

A few months passed and something amazing happened. Both my mother and my stepfather decided to come to church with me one Sunday morning. They dressed Jasmin in her one "nice" outfit we had received from a neighbor and their alarms were set for the ten o' clock service that day.

This was a miracle to me. Not simply because it was out of their schedule and character in every sense, but because it was the first time I started seriously pondering if God was the real deal. No one knew, but I would try to pray by myself. Even with a hesitant heart, I gave it a shot. Ever since I started spending the nights at Grace's house. I would come back home and pray before I fell asleep. I would pray that if there was a God out there, He'd bring my family back together.

I think I wanted to so badly for there to be hope in this world. I gave up on fairy tales and magical creatures long, long ago. But something about prayer was so intriguing. To know that there was a way to release all of the heart's secrets, hurts, joys, and details to a being so free from this dark place was a concept I was fond of. No, I didn't know much; I knew nothing, actually. But I believed in something, and come to think of it, there is a lot to be said about the power of faith. I believed that there was something real in what was happening in Grace's household when they would hold hands and pray. And I firmly believed if my family did what they did for a while, we could have it, too. We could find hot dogs, laughter, and nonsense in our home, too.

***

After seeing the many pamphlets and brochures, my parents cane to church to see what it was all about. We started driving together on Sunday mornings and my stepfather actually began to take work off. It was something so unheard of and so unreal. I liked this. As much as I continued to maintain a skeptical outlook on church, I liked that it was causing something to happen to something that had been so idle for so long. It was changing things. It was moving things.

***

I remember for Jasmin's second birthday, we had many people fit inside our little apartment. We had never really thrown a birthday party before, and to be honest I am not sure if this really counted as one. Most of the people there were too old in my opinion, and one of the women even brought her cat. But these people from church felt the need to throw Jasmin a birthday party and indeed they did such.

I was around ten at this point and for the first time in my life, I saw my mother smile like she meant it. I didn't think this was the circumstance in which I would see this happen. But here we were. Balloons hung all around our crowded kitchen and voices of glee and excitement were bouncing off of our walls. We had hotdogs being grilled outside by the elders of the church and it was good. It was still weird, but it was good, indeed.

Chapter Three:

Eat Your Own Soup

There is this Korean fable that I grew up hearing and it goes something like this: There are these two donkeys, right? And they were friends. They were known to be pretty good friends, actually. Because, you know, there are various levels of relationships one hoofed mammal can have with another. One day, the two friendly donkeys decide to go to a family-owned restaurant somewhere. They both end up ordering the exact same soup. All of a sudden within the story, Donkey #1 becomes quiet. He watches his buddy getting ready to eat his soup but he cannot help but feel as though the server gave Donkey #2 the bowl with the better portion of the chicken, vegetables, and whatever else. He quietly and keenly manipulates Donkey #2 to switch bowls with him, only to realize the bowl that he has before him now is no good at all. He was able to take a closer look at it and much of the broth was unseasoned and the portions, in fact, were smaller. One can gather from this beautifully written story that you should just eat your own soup.

I swear I did not make that up.

I cannot, however, promise how well I translated it over.

Point is:

* Don't steal soup from other donkeys.

…Or as Teddy Roosevelt had sweetly spoken:

"Comparison is the thief of joy."

***

I've played Donkey #1 for most of my life growing up. I think most of us try not to. We want to be satisfied with the given things because more often than not, it is beyond our control. Yet even when we consciously make a point to tell ourselves to be satisfied, we hesitate to stay content. We compare ourselves with others with the intentions of personal growth. Instead, we usually walk away with a deteriorated heart and deteriorating thoughts about others.

Much of my early resentment towards God came from my constant habit of needing to look around at what others were offered in this world. After my seemingly thorough evaluation and having to recognize that I hadn't done anything super atrocious for the God of the world to hate me, I'd come to a conclusion each and every time that He was unfair and He was unjust. It was either that or He didn't exist.

I think that there is a healthy and a very unhealthy way to go about the concept of comparing. Many of us are not ready for it. I also think the more insecure we are about our own lives, the more we tend to compare in an unhealthy way. I could be wrong. But this was pretty accurate about me. Before finding my security in God, I spent most of my time comparing myself with others and before I knew it, irrational jealousy became the epitome of my heart. And jealousy, I have come to find out, is one of the ugliest things known to humankind.

***

Since moving to the United States, I watched my mother go from a highbrow, fur coat-wearing exclusivist to a blue-collar, lower class, dry cleaning lady for a foreign country. I didn't know how much this bothered me and my pride until one day when I went over to my friend Alyssa's in the third grade.

Alyssa and I both rode the yellow school bus and lived a few apartment complexes from one another. We hung out after school and occasionally on the weekends because of our shared interests for Beanie Babies and lime green gel pens.

The first time I went over to Alyssa's, I did not know what to expect. I was a little Asian girl with a Goodwill tote bag to carry my books in and a huge picture of Hello Kitty's face embroidered on my t-shirt by the hands of my mother because we couldn't afford the stuff in the stores. As far as my experiences with interior décor went, it was what I saw in the homes of Disney shows. I remember being super observant during the few times I watched TV in the waiting room with my stepdad for an oil change, but I always thought those types of homes were for superstars.

I did not get out often because of several reasons. For starters, I did not know the language. Secondly, my mother was still acquiring her driver's license, let alone acquiring the idea that we drove on the other side of the road here in the United States and this was supposed to happen while also being seated on other end of the car. There was a lot going on all the time in our household and it was a rare occasion to find myself elsewhere.

The first thing I noticed about Alyssa's home was that they had a doormat. It was eloquently brown and tan in a way where it mocked the brown or tan dirt that would come from the scuffs of my tiny shoes. It had elaborate cursive writing embossed on it and I never had enough patience to dissect what it read. It was as if the doormat heard that I was coming over and decided to twist the letters with extra loops and swirls to test my competence—or lack thereof. I didn't care. I stepped on it with extra vigor and force each and every time because it was the fanciest doormat my feet would ever touch.

Her ceilings were breathtakingly tall and everything was always bright—so bright that my eyes had to look away and readjust its settings. The fruit basket in their kitchen seemed to contain the freshest produces in town and Alyssa's mom always happened to be ready for a special occasion. She smelled like the mall and her hair was big. To me, she appeared to be an adult-sized princess and the two together were sisters who shared secrets about cotton candy and glitter. I had thought Alyssa's family and my family lived in the same apartment complexes. And we did. But their home was without a doubt prettier, cleaner, more interesting, and better.

***

Every time I walked back home from playing at Alyssa's dream house, I thought about their doormat that would greet me in and carefully watch me leave. Before visiting Alyssa's, I never thought about doormats. I never thought about the importance of them, let alone know they were necessary at all. But all of a sudden it hit me how deprived I had been living in a home without a doormat to greet me in and to secure me a nice sendoff each and every time I exited to conquer the world.

I don't know why I was so stuck on the doormat, but I was. I couldn't help it. It was like Alyssa's weird obsession with keeping the original tags on all of her Beanie Babies; I had an obsession with observing every home all of a sudden and measuring their quality and worth by whether or not they had a doormat. And according to my newly vamped quality-scale, my family's home was the lowest of the low. We didn't have a doormat. We didn't even have a basket in our kitchen for fruits.

I remember coming home from Alyssa's one afternoon with an Olive Garden drink in my hand. I trotted along the edges of the sidewalk on my way back and let out a few giggles that came from the depths of my youthful heart. Alyssa's mother had bought us an early dinner and we were allowed to choose anything on the Olive Garden menu. It was fantastic. I got some form of spaghetti; it was the first time I had tried spaghetti outside of our school's cafeteria.

When I walked into our humble home, my mother had come early from work and was folding laundry at the kitchen table. She was sweaty and her eyes were tired. She asked me where I had gotten the drink. I told her Alyssa's mom was cool and that was why she was able to buy me and Alyssa whatever we wanted. She looked at me with a form of puzzlement in her face.

"Why do you have to phrase it like that?" she asked.

"What?" I responded with an overwhelming amount of attitude.

"Am I not 'cool' because I don't get you Olive Garden whenever you want?"

In my adolescent mind, it wasn't rocket science. I thought I had made myself clear enough and there was no need for further discussion. With an irritated voice, I murmured back,

"Mom. Stop. It's not because you *don't;* you and I both know you *can't*. I know it's not your fault. It's just Alyssa's mom's richer and stuff."

"Well if you expect me to say sorry, it's not happening."

"Mom. Why do you have to be this way?" I retorted selfishly, "You make me feel as though everything I do or feel is my fault. Even when it's not my fault that you aren't rich or that I was born into this little home and I had no say in whether or not we have a doormat. It's not fair that I live like this when Alyssa doesn't have to do anything to deserve Olive Garden whenever she wants!"

I knew I wasn't making sense but I didn't care. I was being the ultimate brat who was on a sugar-high and I knew it.

My mother was worn out from work already, but I exhausted her from her energy completely. She carefully placed the towel she was working on and looked into my eyes,

"Are you embarrassed of me?"

I raised my voice at my mother for the first time that day. I didn't know that had it in me. I had no idea why this triggered such a reaction, but it did. I placed my cherished drink on the table and took a big breath,

"Yes! Okay? I admit! Yes I am! I *am* embarrassed of you. I am embarrassed at the way you can't speak like an educated person on this continent you decided to place us in. I am embarrassed that I can't welcome my friends to this home because you don't understand. I hate that you dress as though you have no self-dignity anymore. And I am embarrassed that you think it is okay not to prepare meals for your own daughter just because you work late and I have to pretend that it doesn't bother me. Why am I the one staying home to potty-train Jasmin and why do I have to be hurting because of mistakes *you* made? What's worse it that you know it, too. You know all of this but you won't do anything about it. Yes, mother. I am embarrassed of you. You asked. I answered."

I crossed every threshold. It was bleak and it was loud and it was quiet, all in the same moment. For stepping on such new grounds, the experience should have been reviving and liberating.

But it wasn't. In fact, it was just the opposite.

***

I wish I could tell you that the story between me and my mother becomes delightfully settling and tame after a few good lectures and a round of sharing our feelings. But then I'd be lying to you. I continued to compare my life with my peers' while my mother admittedly compared me to the plethora of other angelic children she would meet throughout her days to come. We were at each other's throats on a daily basis and walls were built in unspeakable directions.

While never showing it, I became utterly jealous of these seemingly do-gooder, no-brainer, brown-nosing kids she would talk about. What I hated more was that I was jealous about it in the first place. I wanted to not care. But I did; it absolutely ate away at me to know I wasn't meeting up to my mother's standards. I despised that my mother seemed to like them more than me and this made me want to be everything she didn't want me to be while somehow making her proud of me at the same time. I didn't know what they had that I didn't other than the fact that they probably lived with a mother who would take them to Olive Garden and understood their words far better than my mother ever would try with mine.

***

At the end of fifth grade, Alyssa told me that she and her mother were moving away. She came from a broken family like mine and said that it was going to become whole again. Her mom had found a new man and Alyssa said she would soon have to change her last name to his. We giggled because attaching her first name with this man's last name sounded funny and unfamiliar. They were moving into a house three hours away and it was supposed to be an exciting thing. But Alyssa spoke with sadness in her voice. We became great friends throughout the years and she was worried about finding new people in her neighborhood to talk about Beanie Babies and green gel pens with. In the midst of hugging and saying goodbye in the presence of her fancy doormat, Alyssa looked at me and took my hand,

"Ji, can I tell you a secret?"

"Sure."

"I sometimes wish I had your life."

"What?" I laughed and felt shy.

"Yeah. Like, I never wanted to admit this, but I have always been super jealous of you. I hope you know how lucky you are."

"...Why in the world would *you* be jealous of *me*?"

"Well, for one, you have a little sister."

"What?"

"Yeah. I'm always so bored by myself. Mom's usually gone these days with her boyfriend—I mean, my stepdad, and there's no one to play with. I also like that you can eat whenever you want. Mom's boyfriend looks at me in a mean way when I don't sit right or eat all of the stuff at the right time at the table. It's scary. He always talks about cavities, too."

"Oh..." I awkwardly said aloud, "You know, you probably don't know this. But I have three cavities already, see?" I opened my mouth wide enough for people in China to have a clear sight of it all, "Yeah, and I don't really know how to tie my shoes yet. So that's kind of embarrassing."

"What?"

"Are you still jealous of me?"

"Yeah."

"Why?"

"Because you have a little sister. And straight hair."

***

The thing about comparing is that more often than not, the subject is hardly the matter. We simply fixate our attention and place our concern on something that is different than what we currently attain. I'm making it a big deal because it is. Whether it's two children, women on *The Bachelor*, or political figures fighting over airtime on national television. The concept of comparing so easily becomes a way to flaunt our immaturity and lack of knowing how to live intentionally. This is me trying to blow it into proportion. From the moment we are old enough to understand that life is not fair, we willfully make a choice to weigh our hearts down by filling it with jealousy. We have to realize that this is a big deal because it's our lives we are talking about. It's the time we often correlate with money and other seemingly glorified things. We waste it and we have an option to prevent this tragedy from prolonging. We don't have to be held captive by envy and greed. We don't have to sit around and shamefully fantasize about the what-if's while the things that are already firm in our possession become forgotten, outdated and soon expired. It's sad because we have a choice, but we neglect the better option due to our selfish impulse to look better.

The truth is, we compare and become jealous of what others have because we do very little to be thankful for what we do have. Even in elementary school, I am confident to say that I was well aware of my mother's inevitable circumstances. It wasn't her fault, not completely. But it didn't seem to be mine either. I could have chosen to be angry with God but that didn't seem to resolve. So I kept blaming my mother because I had fingers to point and they needed something to aim at. But I think I knew all along that sometimes there was indeed no one to blame. Yet, my own wants and needs overpowered my awareness of truth.

Jealousy doesn't just overtake our vision; it blinds us. Instead of being thankful, we place useless and wasted efforts into loathing everything about the imperfections in our lives. Broadly speaking, we forget to eat our own soup. We fail to see what is right in front of us...the things of which many people never even had or will ever have. Because of our desire to tend only to ourselves, we neglect to see others' jealous hearts gazing upon our very own bowl, if you will. We feed others' jealousy while sustaining our own. It is a big web of ugly and we end up hurting innocent people along the way. When we fall into this dangerous trap of endless monotony, we are all losers in a game the devil loves to play.

***

One day after school, I came home to my mother doing laundry again. There was an Arby's bag sitting on the counter along with a drink. I eyed the unfamiliar sight and looked back at my mother. She then walked over to the bag and placed it in my hands.

"These are not the ones I wanted to get you," she explained, "But the woman at the other end of a speaker did not understand what I ordered because of my broken English."

I imagined my little South Korean mother interacting with an irritated drive-thru worker as she failed to make a fast transaction with her words and her money. The sheer thought of her being disrespected and misunderstood pained my insides.

"Mom. Why did you get this? We can't afford this."

She looked at me with repentance in her eyes, "I know it's not Olive Garden, but I just want you to know you deserve it." This broke me. I didn't deserve it. I thought I did up until this moment. It was a gift too good for me to take because I knew I had broken her, too.

***

I have a feeling that when we find it so easy to compare our things, our lives, and ourselves with what it is not, we insult God and the things that He has prepared for us. I believe that His heart breaks...not because He loses anything, but because we do. I could be wrong. But I just have this ridiculously urgent feeling that we should stop. We should stop wanting more just for ourselves. We should stop looking around and instead, look up and be glad. There are always going to be doormats and fruit baskets lingering in this world for us to attain at a later time; these things are hardly the point. We don't really know how to be thankful because we live in a world that sells us the misleading idea that we never have it good enough, henceforth advertisements that urge us to get *more*. And it works. We keep getting more, only to become thirsty for more again. The twisted part about it all is that, like Donkey #1, we won't be satisfied. We won't. It's true. So-and-so's soup is just as cold and broth-less as yours. And it always will be. You can tell me all you want about how your boat or your new boyfriend makes you the happiest of all the land...but your boat will eventually rust and your new boyfriend doesn't mean anything unless there is an eternal commitment. Someone else's boat and someone else's boyfriend isn't the answer either. Happiness from the things that this world provides is temporary. We just choose not to believe this because we don't have enough room in our hearts because it's occupied with envy. But these things that we reach so desperately for are but dust and quicksand. I don't believe that happiness in itself is what our hearts are thirsty for. If it were the case, we would eventually stop wanting more. We would no longer compare or be jealous.

I think we are covertly dying to find *joy*.

Here is a secret. When we do not have gratitude in our hearts, we do not have the prerequisite of joy. To be grateful is to stop comparing in this incessant and unproductive way in which we do. Joy, I have learned, is free and priceless all at the same time. Joy comes from honest and genuine contentment of the *now*. I believe many of us secretly know this but we won't shoot for joy. Why? Because of yet another wall shamelessly standing tall in our hearts. This wall is called pride. And it takes courage to tear down. This wall wasn't built all on our own, either. We had the help of this world as it uses tactics like corrupted societies and tainted media telling us we are never sufficient enough without certain things. It is the devil's favorite trait. This thick and heavy pride in our hearts is difficult to detect because it has injected lies within us throughout the years, and this wall with its lies can and will ruin us.

Joy is an overflow from within, not an absorption of anything our bodies can eat, touch, buy, win, or see. Essentially, the most joyful person should and would be satisfied with absolutely nothing in his or her bowl. It is the fact that this person has discovered that there is something to be sai

Chapter Four:
The 4x4

One of the greatest life lessons I learned while growing up came from my participation in our high school's track and field team. I was a sprinter, and there was no doubt about it either. I thrived off of the immediate adrenaline rush and exerting it all at once. I had the tight runner's thighs, short speedy legs, and the concept of endurance was nowhere near my vocabulary. Did I ever admit that? No way. Nor did I really need to. I ran to finish quickly and to feel the intense breeze whiz past my ears as the noise marvelously clashed with the crowd cheering wildly near the finish line. I did not understand my teammates who ran long distance races. I respected them like crazy. But I didn't care to understand them.

I was an overzealous freshman running varsity for all of my favorite short distances and I fantasized about breaking records by the time this track and field career was kaput. I could not tell you whom we were running against or where it was in the season, but I do recall it was a home meet. It was nearing the end and we were neck and neck with the opposite team. As I was putting my warm-ups and taking off my spikes, I noticed Coach approaching me from the other side of the track.

"Ji, I think we're gonna need ya again," he breathed out as he jogged on over.

"What do you mean, Coach?"

He could hardly get his words out because he was hustling from one end of the curve to the other, "Amanda is injured. We think she might have twisted somethin' but we're definitely not usin' her for the next event. We're gonna need 'ya. I'll see you by the blocks in five."

The next event was the 4x400 meter relay, also known as the 4x4. This relay was always the last event before counting the points and it was also the most intense thing ever. This was because it was usually was the race we counted on to make it or break it. Even though the sport in itself was a team activity, each of these races were spotlights to particular participants. If one was to mess up—especially the last race—it wasn't a team thing, it really was an individual thing.

I started putting my spikes back on and thought about what Coach said. He said I was taking place of Amanda. Amanda ran the anchor leg of our 4x4. This meant she was the last of the four runners to complete the race. She did not pass the relay baton off to anyone. Amanda was literally the person we would ultimately count on to "bring it home". Except now it was me. I had never competed in the distance of 400 meters. For those of you who don't run, that is once around a standard high school track. All together as a relay team, we would be running a mile. It is such a bizarre distance because although it is not long, it is an incredible amount to sprint the whole span. Some might even go as to say that the 400-meter run in itself is one of the most difficult races.

The five minutes shortly passed and before I knew it, I was loosening up by the blocks, preparing to hear the buzzing wind like I always have. The race began with what seemed as though was the loudest gunshot of the entire meet and my heart was already pounding louder than the voices coming from through from the announcers. I had never been so nervous for a race before. I was conditioned to being confident in my element. This, however, was not my element; this was twice as long as what my heart had been adjusted to.

***

I won't even try to describe to you how ugly I had finished our 4x4. I mean, we made it into second place. But there were also only two teams. It was hands-down the most difficult physical work I had ever done in my life. My legs gave out after the first straightaway and the rest was history. I almost wish that there had been someone recording it because I am confident I was going backwards at one point. It literally felt like I was running in place and the ruthless track was slipping beneath my pointless spikes.

"You know what you could have used? Endurance."

These were the words of Coach after that meet. I will never forget them. This wasn't the first time he had mentioned the need of endurance to me. He had always talked of how I needed to put in my minutes, hours, and days toward conditioning my heart for endurance during our off-season practices. But this time, he didn't tell me this again to sound like a broken record. He was telling this to me to make sure I was awakened and could hear with new ears. It was almost like a nicer form of implying, *I told you so.* But, indeed, his words stuck this time because I had to learn it the hard way and tasted how vital and true they were.

I share this, not because I want you to sign me up for the next nearest marathon, but because I have found myself in this very position time and time again in my faith journey. As a person who finds faith to be her most important priority, I often catch myself running dry when I am stretched far beyond my element. If endurance, indeed, is something that can be practiced with our physical beings, I believe it can also be practiced with our spiritual hearts.

***

After several years of attending church with me in the fifth grade, my mother had a certain prayer that she would try out and share every so often on our Sunday drives back home. She'd tell me she was praying to God that He would bless us with a house.

It was one of the most ridiculous things I had ever heard come out of my mother's mouth but I never had the guts to tell her. We had lived in the same apartment complex since we first migrated over to the United States and as far as I knew, this was the place my mother and my stepfather would forever live in. They simply had no qualifications or capabilities for anything more. It may sound faithless, but that's only because I was. They were making money in a foreign country hardly being able to speak the language, let alone understand how to make a house payment.

As soon as my mother decided Jesus was someone worth while, she began to pray this fervent prayer and in the duration, I couldn't help but pity her. Real things were bought with real money and real money came from real work. I just didn't understand why she was stuck in this fantasy world that this persistent prayer would be effective for something so monumental. It was impossible and that was the reality of life that I knew.

Two years in, our family's dry cleaning business flirted with bankruptcy and in the meantime, rent for the apartment continued to rise by impressive increments. I would wake up to my mother at our kitchen counter with her hands folded and head bowed down every morning before I left for school and I would simply shake my head. We never approached the option or the likelihood of owning a house. In fact, we took giant leaps away from the possibility year after year.

As much as I wanted to understand where my mother was coming from, I could not help but wonder if God was going to think that her request was a selfish prayer. I didn't know God super well even then but I was fully conscious of the fact that He wasn't fond of greedy people. My mother would ask me to partake in the prayer for our family to be granted by a house and I always nodded but never actually did.

Several more years went by and there was nothing different about our circumstances. I was entering my junior hear of high school and by this point, I was so indulgent in my own emotions regarding things outside of the home that I had no idea where we stood financially. I pretended not to care while internally counting down the days when I left for college to escape this mess, then came one of the most humbling phone calls of my life.

I was coming out of track practice with my loud teammates as we sported many things neon when my mother rang. She sounded calm and collected while the words coming out of her mouth threw me for a loop.

"Ji-Hyun, I won't be home 'til late tonight. I know that's nothing too out of the ordinary but I just thought you'd like to know this time it's because your stepdad and I are going to sign some documents for our new house."

"…What."

***

My mother quickly became what many would call a prayer warrior. And the funny thing about it is that she was the unlikeliest candidate. I think God has a knack for that. Actually, I believe He does this for a very good purpose. Life and its people are not meant to be predictable; they're meant to be an adventure and a constant wonder.

On our move-in day, I constantly caught myself staring at my mother. I just couldn't believe it. I took her by the shoulder as she was walking back into the house to grab her purse,

"Mom, how have I not seen you freak out yet? This is crazy! How did that money come rolling in so sudden? And what? I just don't even...?"

"There was no money; the house was a gift," she replied.

"You're saying someone gave us this house? Are you serious?"

She nodded and smiled, "More or less."

"Mom, did you see this coming? Who were they?"

"I think always knew," she said, "And you wouldn't know them well. They are new friends to us. But even before we met the generous people who gave us this offer. I'd say I always knew."

She was being all mystical and I had enough of it.

I looked at her with discontent, "Mom, isn't that kind of cocky?"

"No," she said, "It's confidence. To be cocky would mean that I thought I could do things on my own and that this was about me. This is nothing about me or my capabilities. This is my confidence in God. I am nothing without Him, but all things are possible with Him. You should know that, Ji-Hyun. Why are you so surprised?"

***

The first thing she installed in our house was a prayer room. It was a small and snug sanctuary dedicated specifically for meditation and prayer. The next thing she did was go to every thrift shop and outlet store nearby to furnish two guestrooms. She didn't even have a bed in her own bedroom yet.

I guess never really asked her why she wanted a house. I always thought it was an ego thing. Come to find out, it was a dream behind a dream. She revealed to me her long-awaited idea of hosting other foreign students in a pleasant home so that they could experience the lessons I learned while studying in the United States. She said she had a hard time admitting it to me, but that she thought I was able to discover important truths to life that every kid should have an opportunity to learn by living through them. She thought with this, she could even bring them to know Jesus, too. That was her ultimate goal. She said God gave her this revelation a while ago. She simply wanted a house as a tool and a resource, not as prized possession or something to boast about. She prayed even in times of trial because she knew what she was working for and she was certain of her Coach.

I never knew that kind of faith.

My mother's heart had practiced endurance. She was changing and enduring, majestically and undoubtedly.

***

As much as runners don't just wake up one day with an incredible ability to endure, maybe it really does takes practice for our spiritual hearts, too. And even then, we must keep conditioning otherwise we will wear ourselves out. We need to pray persistently and ridiculously everyday if we truly do believe we are connecting with a God who is in control. We need to pray, not only for the sake of today, but for the times when the unexpected occurs. It is not to say that we pray with an anxious heart, but one that knows it will be held in the palm of God's hands when we do have to run things like the 4x4. We know we will be ready. We know we will endure and see the prize at the end of the race.

The old me used to pray for comfort. And I did it whenever it was convenient. I never actually expected Him to do anything, so I never gave Him much of a chance to move in my life. I just thought He was more of an unconditional listener when I felt lonely or bitter about everyone else. I limited God to be just a good friend. Yes, He was a friend, but He was also a Father. And this righteous Father never lets His children down. He always provides, protects, and loves surprising His precious children.

It is said that the Christian life is not an easy one. And I am a firm believer of that. Life, the fullness of its meaning, is no walk in the park and there are trials all around. But when a curveball comes crashing in, I hope my heart knows how to endure. I hope I don't give out early because I didn't prepare myself for these unforeseen challenges. I hope that I do put in my valuable minutes, hours, and days of practice in conditioning my heart for endurance in hopes to stay strong at the end. I hope to be more like my mother. I also never thought I would find myself saying such words. God truly does change people for the good...for the better.

***

I still consider myself a sprinter; it's just who I am. I like running fast. I still like buzzing through forests and hearing my heart chase after my breath. But I practice long distances every so often. It doesn't come easy for me and I don't particularly find it fun. It is out of my element and I am uncomfortable with it. But I've been doing it more and more often because I have come to realize that shooting things out of our comfort zone is usually when life really begins.

Chapter Five:
Prayer Works

The first time I ever went to the casino, I went with a pack of semi-proficient guys and my not-so-proficient friend Jess. It was a sporadic decision after a wedding up in northern Michigan and we had a bit too much sparkling juice to stay calm and collected inside of a stuffy hotel lounge all night.

When we were initially invited, Jess and I looked at each other, giggling insecurely because we didn't want to admit that we had never gambled before. Was that something we should have been embarrassed about? Probably not. But at the time, we were the minority of the party. Also, we didn't want to look like complete party poopers, so we tagged along.

As we entered the building, one of the guys slipped me a wad of some single bills and told me not to sweat it. He then gave me a friendly nudge of encouragement and wished me luck.

They didn't waste much time and soon dispersed to their own line of moneymakers while Jess and I quickly found ourselves standing in what seemed to be the eye of a neon, smoky hurricane called the casino. It reeked a spellbinding mist of wistful infatuation and lustful addiction. With the few dollars I had clenched in my hand, Jess and I ventured on the most unsatisfying two and a half hours of our inexperienced, amateur, gambling lives.

Aimless and incompetent, we went up to this man with an official casino badge and a nametag that read, "Ronnie Ron". We told him we had no clue how to play or win or whatever it was that we were supposed to do and he gave us the look I often received from my teachers in elementary school when I'd ask in my broken English if I could use the bathroom.

Caring and pitying, Ronnie Ron advised us to try out the slots that had the giant green clovers hovering on top of the machines. They were a few rows down from where we stood. He also said he'd encourage us to try out the tables but they were pretty busy in the current hour. We submitted to his words and headed over to the clovers but this was also because we probably could not have found these tables he spoke of even if they we tried.

With slight mischief and excitement in our eyes, Jess and I took our seats in front of the massive screens that flashed spinning numbers and images of tacky clovers. We looked at one another, shrugged, and both inserted a single dollar into the slits.

Jess' machine did nothing the first round while mine made a few fun beeping noises and informed me that I just earned eighty cents. I had no idea how I did that.

"…I have no idea how I did that!" I innocently exclaimed.

"What the heck? Where's my eighty cents?" Jess wrinkled her nose and pulled her hair back in a ponytail, "I'm trying again."

And so she did. I did, too. We kept inserting the dollar bills and waited around for the machines to sing us some songs and make a few more beeping noises. Every once in a while, it would even show us photos of some animated Irish woman. I literally had no idea what was going on, nor did I understand the numbers on the bottom of the screen. I also wasn't sure what caused my machine to think it owed me eighty more cents than I put in, but I felt pretty good about it.

***

At the end of the night, Jess and I walked away a dollar and seven cents richer. This was a good thing because at one point, we went negative by twenty-something bucks. As soon as we broke even and played a few more rounds of slots to say that we actually won something (the whopping dollar and seven cents), a small and irritated voice in our heads told us to walk away and find the guys so that we could head back to the hotel and get some food.

***

The reason I share this pathetic story with you is because I cannot think of a better way to describe how my prayer life looked before I decided to take it seriously. Even with the recent testimonies of my family's circumstances, I still couldn't inhale the concept wholly. I was an aimless spirit, wandering and listening to what everyone else had to say when I was seeking answers from ones who were no more practiced or successful at it than me. When I would throw a prayer out there, I expected those clovers to line up all across the board in my life because this was how God had been advertised to me. He was supposed to appreciate the amount I offered and give back something suitable for me to work with. If and when He didn't, I would get agitated, feeling robbed of my time and cheated as a player of a system that was obviously corrupt and built to put me to shame.

Regardless, I kept on praying anyway. I thought I could play God like a slot machine; I didn't have to invest much but if somehow this really was real, I wanted to make sure I kept my foot in the door. I never actually proclaimed that I didn't believe in God in fear that this voyeuristic, all-knowing God would hear it with micro-hearing devices implanted in every carpet square or something. Yet, I never openly admitted I was a follower of Jesus either because I didn't want to be the fool when somebody proved that we were actually controlled by aliens or something. I just didn't want to be in the wrong. I wanted to play it safe. I wanted to rightly play or win or whatever it was that we were supposed to do.

***

My biggest ordeal regarding prayer was that I didn't know where people went to go to learn and get better at it. Was there even such a concept or practice? No one taught me how and no one ever talked about it either. Did some people step into this world with full knowledge and connection to the spiritual realm while beginners like me had to learn the hard way? That didn't seem fair. Or was this world that we lived in but a massive casino where we all drifted worthlessly, trying to connect to a gambling god and left our hope to sheer luck and the few dollar bills we were able to scrounge off of others?

The thing with prayer is that it's beyond our logic, our tricks, our understanding. It has to be. It is the medium used to communicate to a God who is beyond our world. What we have to get over is that there is no bonus button or a cheatable system to it. It's not a system at all. It is a divine conversation. As unattainable as God is for us to conceptualize, so is the art and science of prayer.

Although my capability to understand the inner workings of prayer has not changed, I've come to be convinced of this much:

Our God is not a gambling god.

He is undeniably listening, and prayer works.

***

Growing up, my family never had health insurance because of its price. This was detrimental to the ways we would inevitably treat our bodies because the cost of simple living outweighed the need to take care of our sicknesses. We let this slip for a while but when I entered high school, we couldn't hold back anymore.

My mother began to grow a mole on the bridge of her nose and for the time being, we made nothing of it. It wasn't until my friend's father who was a doctor noticed it one day and asked if we had gotten it checked out. I told him it was not a big deal and he looked at me with a serious worry. He diagnosed it and considered it to be cancerous. Relaying this information to my mother was one of the most difficult things to do as the doctor and I calculated treatment costs and confirmed that it was out of our capabilities to pay.

***

People talk about how the days in which Jesus walked the earth is no longer applicable to our lives today. I have had many friends say that miracles cannot happen and that prayers are practiced by the ignorant. I have also heard many say that only real, tangible work produces growth, goods, and change—not prayer.

It says in the Bible that Jesus is the same yesterday, today and forever. He did things like turning water into wine and healing the blind with His spit and the very dirt from the ground. My mother took these words of Scripture to heart and began praying over her mole in Jesus' name. Three times per day, she'd place her right hand over where her cancer was. I thought the mole was making my desperate mother mad. She kept claiming that there was power in Jesus' name and she was confident He could heal, even if our pockets couldn't suffice the funds. This was still early on in our walk of faith together as a family and I personally found it to be a bit weird. And by *a bit,* I mean a lot. The house was one thing but this was completely out of my league. I'd awkwardly walk the other way as I would pretend I did not see that she was being absolutely ludicrous.

"Well what do you think prayer is for?" My mother asked once. I didn't know how to answer, so I kept walking away as I always did.

***

When leaving for my freshman year of college, I observed my mother's collarbone glisten outside as we stood at the end of our driveway. It never used to protrude from her body the way it began to do so. *She's losing weight*, I thought.

I navigated my eyes upward toward her face. It sure had been a while since I last *looked* at her. The wrinkles around her eyes landed on her face so unexpectedly and intrusively. They were a physical collection of her trials and agonies, the pain I had never known. For the first time in a very long time, I felt something in my heart for my mother. I so badly wished I could do heal her, but all I could say was that I would "pray" for her as I drove away in my Volkswagen and waved a sorry goodbye.

As I began my classes, our family continued to struggle. I was doing just fine finding my own jobs to pay for the needs to get by and networking to uproot myself from the life I once knew. I was finally able to live my dream of escaping the past and planting my feet on something I could be proud about. But as I'd pick up phone calls from Jasmin and she'd describe our mother's coughs and spoke of my stepfather having to come home later and later, I felt suffocated by guilt as I debated dropping out on a daily basis. I wasn't quite sure what that would have done, but I didn't seem to be doing anything to help. Yet in her circumstances, my mother picked up a second job as a housekeeper at a hotel in downtown Grand Rapids in hopes that this bit could help for all that was happening. I felt helpless and sad, but mainly mad at God. This was because it was then when I thought that perhaps I should have stuck with becoming a doctor — that financially stable "leader" — who my sick mother had always dreamt for me to be. As queasy as the idea made me, I thought maybe then we wouldn't live so powerlessly. Maybe then I could help cure her. Perhaps God didn't care about my personal dreams. Maybe He just liked to poke fun at me like He always had.

***

I did not see my family again until a few months down the road. I do not know how to say this next part without tears, but to my absolute surprise, I saw my mother's face and the mole was gone.

It literally disappeared.

I asked her how we were able to afford such a surgery.

She said she never went in.

With confusion and awe, I questioned what she was implying.

"Jesus healed me, Ji-Hyun," my mother humbly replied.

"But what do you mean by that?" I urgently demanded.

"After the ninety-first time I prayed over the bridge of my nose, it was completely gone," she said.

I didn't believe her. But I had no choice. My mother, because of her holy transformation from the inside out, is the reason my faith is what it is today. I was actually staring at a real life miracle and it happened to be my mother. She had nothing to gain by telling me a lie about such a matter. I just did not want to believe it to be true because it completely thrashed everything I had ever known and blew these preconceived notions away. I didn't think these actual "miracles" happen. I never thought that I was the type of person who needed proof for faith. But here it was. And I began to believe all over again.

As humbling as it was, this was also when Jesus truly allowed me to realize that He didn't need me to do anything. He was God. He could and would overcome anything. If His people simply believed, He didn't need them to achieve a certain point in their financial careers or a threshold of their pride to bless them well. Faith was the key. Jesus had it covered; He knew all along. He most certainly was still powerful and He was just as present as He was when He walked here years ago.

I was brought to my knees and I laughed and cried. I laughed and I cried like a child as I gazed at my healthy mother with wonder.

***

During this short period of time I visited home, I was able to meet with an old friend. Cara is the kind of girl who never takes your opinion of anything to be accurate unless she went and tried it for herself. Very skeptical and very clever. She was also my partner in crime for every senior prank pulled at schools we didn't even go to. As we sat on the lawn chairs displayed outside of Lowe's, Cara asked how my mother was doing. I told her all that had happened and she didn't speak for a long time. As I played around with the price tags on the chair I was sitting in, Cara finally chimed,

"So you believe that kind of stuff?"

"It's not just that I want to, Cara. I have to. There are only so many times you see the impossible happen before your eyes until you just gotta say, 'Okay. That's it. I believe.'"

"You know that makes you look crazy, right?"

I smiled at her, "If being crazy is to finally know the reason why you live...then yeah, I'm absolutely crazy."

Cara shook her head and said we could still be friends as long as I didn't throw Bibles at her. So I didn't. I never threw anything at her, but I did say this,

"You reap what you sow, Cara. And once you see that the reaping is worth the sowing, you reap again."

***

The thing I've come to know is that to follow Jesus is to take the entire Bible for what it is and what it says it is. All of it. Not just the fragments that apply for our circumstances and the verses that make more sense to our society. We take all of it or we have nothing at all. It's the whole truth or a complete lie in which we deceitfully live.

My mother's miracle with her cancerous mole was not the only drastic physical miracle Jesus bestowed upon our family through prayer. My stepfather had been a chain smoker since he could first count money to buy the packs and much of his addiction was due to emotional turmoil from the things he had to grow up with. It seriously affected Jasmin's health while she was born and it truly was appalling for our family dynamic. But because of his embedded habit, he could not simply let it go. It was yet another expense for our family and it was a lousy one. Although we tried everything we could in our resources to help, nothing could cut it. His stubbornness in his addiction was impeccable and the ways he would attempt to hide it never fooled anyone.

After our family first decided to attend church together years ago, we placed his addiction to be one of our top prayers on our list. Well, we said we would one Sunday morning when the message at church was once about praying as a family. But we never actually did. We were still very much apathetic toward God. We scribbled this prayer list on a piece of paper but I don't think any of us took it home. When I left for college and God began to really rock my world, I know now for fact that He began to rock my family's as well. Not until over three years later did my mother tell me that they had begun to fervently pray over my stepfather's condition. Without knowing, we happened to choose the same mornings for five consecutive months to pray for him. Two years ago, my stepfather quit smoking. Just like that. It was out of the blue and we never questioned it. He said he all of a sudden did not have the craving for it anymore and it also happened to be around the same time he joined a men's Bible study at church.

It's honestly crazy, the way God works with time. In His perfect and purposeful timing, God was orchestrating our family to grow together in Him all along, regardless of disposition. But what I had to realize was that it wasn't just about healing my mother or my stepfather. It wasn't just about giving us hope to know that we can physically revive, thanks to Jesus. It was the fact that He answered prayers so timely to let us know that He not only listens, but He cares about the depths of our hearts. And deep down inside, I desperately still wanted my family to just come together...to find ourselves praying together at dinner tables and laughing because we could. And we could not help but to do so when in the midst of His answered prayers.

***

Every now and then, I think about to what my friends would say in terms of miracles and prayer and how it negates the need for work. I don't consider what my parents had done throughout their years of healing to be anything but work. They persevered and diligently prayed. They took their valuable time and efforts to get on their knees and confess before God who is in all control that they could not handle the cancers, the addictions, and the hardships of this world alone. They welcomed Him into their lives.

They were willing to be vulnerable.

They made a point to let go of their pride.

If you ask me, that takes more work than many of us would ever want to take up.

In the Bible, it says that those who do not do their portion of work do not deserve to be fed. I don't believe individuals who believe in the power of prayer to be lazy. Nor do I believe they are the type who ought not to be fed. I think they work with an abundant amount of faith that is rewarded by God who pours His blessings on His people when we seek Him first. In our modern world, we're so clouded with simulated comfort and jaded with irrational worry. We cast it upon our luck and chances while we are missing the point that God is beyond anything our own hands could ever deal.

***

Maybe the reason why my prayer life was so uncertain and insecure is because I didn't want to do the work. I prayed hard only when I felt the need for God and let it all go the moment I felt competent again. I was lazy in the one thing that I most certainly should have been working hard in. It was as though the moment a woman at the casino won the jackpot next to me, I would try again but only threw out a prayer that seemed to be worth twenty dollars because I just needed God to be sure that He understood how badly I wanted my prayer answered.

While observing and witnessing the vastly growing faith of my parents, I have come to realize faith isn't something to bargain with. God doesn't cheapen our lives in such ways. He just loves. And He loves hard. It has nothing to do with chance or luck. In fact, I refrain from using those words anymore. I choose to see that prayer—like other forms of communication—is based on trust, commitment, hard work, and clarity. I won't ever go to a casino again. I'd much rather invest in something that is guaranteed to stick. Something worth my work and effort. Something that won't steal, but rather multiply with provision and goodness.

***

The very base of who I am shifted after these miraculous series of events. I cannot see the face value of items and the money they are worth with anymore. I used to be the girl in high school who budgeted by comparing everything I purchased with the simple calculation of, "how many pairs of BKE jeans is this worth?" But when you witness something as jaw-dropping and radical that no money can suffice, all else seems to fall short. One cannot see price anymore. Things are priceless with God. It almost seems silly to live abundantly in wealth, because now I cannot help but see it as excess. If I truly need something, I have God. And maybe I am wrong but I think maybe this is why our world shuns the idea of miracles. Because we make a point to have all of what we need so that we are not desperate for them. When we are not desperate for help outside ourselves, we bathe with pride, which ultimately rots and spoils us to our very core.

I prefer to feel my heartbeat. I want to know that I am leaning on God because I have come to find that it is a radically exciting way to live. I learn to feel the edge, I learn to balance better, and my senses awaken. This kind of living gives me hope and faith for all things to come, because even when I can't, He endures. I don't have to live in a pathetic eye of a neon, smoky hurricane of a slot machine lifestyle. It is not a shaky life of uncertainty with Jesus. In Him, it's no luck. In Him, I am able to have confidence. And if you ask me, I'd rather leap dangerously with faith than be safe and never make it off the ground.

You see, we are not in the position to complain about not being able to "feel" God when we're not walking toward Him. We ought to live our lives and dare to do crazy things for Him and to better ourselves. If we do this with a heart stripped of pride and drenched in unexplainable faith, I promise, we can see that prayer works. We will realize that we've been putting Him in a box this entire time. No wonder so many of us privileged enough to do things like read these books complain about boredom. We're too scared to live by faith. We are living in the fluffy middle of it all and when we're there, we forget to see how exciting it is to feel something real. We forget to grasp that this life is a miraculous one and to live boldly in Jesus' name is actually the safest of them all.

***

A while ago, I was hanging out with my good friend Charlie. Every time Charlie says a joke, he preludes it with, "...now, this might only be funny because I'm an engineer..." and he's usually right. He's too brilliant for his own good and he also happens to love God more than anything.

It was a relaxed night after we both had long days of work and as we allowed ourselves to rest on a dusty living room floor, I looked to Charlie and said,

"Char, you are one of the most logical and mathematical thinkers I know. Doesn't it become difficult to upkeep your belief in such a mysterious God?"

Charlie took his necessary time to swish the question around in his mouth, and as he spoke, he gave me one of the most comforting insights I had ever heard, "Of course, Ji. But you know, I don't think it's meant to be an easy thing. Because then the joy of discovering His existence over and over again would dwindle away to nothing. The gift would be gone. I like to think about how the smartest people on this earth at one point believed that the world was flat until years later they realized perhaps they had not discovered everything there was to discover. The fact that there's always more happening beyond what we are able to tell is a mystery in itself and because of that, I do not feel foolish at all to believe in God. Actually, I find it to be more logical than anything I had ever studied."

***

I don't think we have to understand it all. Kind of like the beauty of a rainbow or the heights of the universe. Except with God, it's not a trick of the eye or a systematic deception. He is truth and truth is unshakable. Maybe it is okay to be still and to know something beyond our reason is holding this world together. Maybe it's good to humbly live in faith and be certain of the undefined. Maybe this is why we must pray. Our actions alone are caused by our limited reason and simple understanding. But what God can do for us through prayer and supplication is beyond reason and far beyond understanding.

We pray because we can. We pray because it works.

Chapter Six:
Relationship Status

Three years ago, I went to a women's leadership retreat for a job I had at the time and one of the forums focused on the topic of maintaining important relationships and how to upkeep them even in the midst of our busy millennial lives. The main speaker during my session kept her bullet points very simple and according to her latest studies, these were the essentials to remember:

- *You must place sacrificed work and time into it*
- *You can only change yourself, not the other person*
- *All quarrels stem from your personal fear or pain*

Perhaps we were supposed to be applying these rules to our relationships with our co-workers or future clients, but all I could think about was God during her presentation as I sat there in my squeaky plastic chair. This was only because earlier that week, I had a ridiculous conversation with a kid named Andrew while in line at our Guitar Center about a shirt I was wearing.

It was a weekday and I had just come from the gym before entering the store to pick up a few things for a friend. As I waited in by the counter with my hands full, a fifteen-year-old version of Adam Levine with electric blue braces stood behind me and impudently poked me in the back.

"What's that mean?"

I turned around and found him now pointing at my chest. I looked down at his index finger and slapped his hand away from my boobs as I lost grip of everything I was holding.

"Excuse me?" I said.

"What's that mean on your back?"

To my surprise, I was sporting an old youth group T-shirt from the same year we were all singing *The World's Greatest* by R. Kelly. With that being said, I had no recollection of what my shirt read or what event it was even from.

"Well, what's it say on my back?" I asked, feeling kind of dumb.

"It says, 'it's a relationship, not a religion'...and it's in awful Comic Sans. You really gotta work on your design skills."

"I didn't make the shirt."

"Okay, fine. But what's it mean? Is it about Christianity? How's it not a religion? Y'all are obsessed about some god and so, you, like, worship it and have crazy rituals for it and stuff. Sounds like a religion to me."

I was tempted to grab this kid by the ear and tell him that I just got done running seven miles and I still had fast blood running through my veins, enough to take him for a lap.

But he wasn't completely wrong. He had me stumped. I was pretty tired and the more I thought about it, the less I could make sense of it all. This really was a pretty bogus marketing strategy, especially for God. I wasn't quite sure what the differentiation was. I also wasn't sure what it meant to have a "relationship" with Jesus. I could technically go around saying this about anything. I could have a relationship with my mailman. My dreams. My laptop. A stray cat. What made this claim about Jesus any more or less true, let alone significant? I remember shaking the kid's hand, finding out his name was Andrew, and telling him he should go into philosophy in college. I also ended up buying his guitar picks for him that day so he didn't think that every absent-minded, sweaty, Asian chick out there were as bizarre as me.

To be honest, I wasn't quite sure if I considered myself to be the religious or spiritual type. This is because I wasn't even sure what that meant. I didn't know what I was inferring when carrying these words on my back and this was what I had been twisting and turning about for the days to follow while here I was, staring at the three bullet points scribbled on a white board regarding how to maintain relationships.

If I was supposed to have a "relationship" with God or this man named Jesus, I didn't really know how to maneuver through any of these concepts with someone who walked the earth years before I was born. But aside from critical thinking and basic reasoning, I was certain about one thing: I did have personal fears and pain regarding the concept of God and life in itself. I just didn't know that they played a part yet.

***

When I first decided to attend Hope College, the Christian attribute was an element I was unsure of. The institution was located in Holland, Michigan, less than thirty minutes away from home, and nothing about it was absolutely thrilling to me. If I am downright honest, I only found it to be a decent idea in the case that if I realized partying in college was something I wanted to get into, it would be twice as difficult for me because I would have an extra hurdle to jump over. I thought this was a shrewd play on my part because I had three Excel spreadsheets worth of planning I had done of what I wanted my future to look like. The typical college scene of drinking and flirting with excited boys was not going to cut it for my route to becoming a world-famous artist and the queen of England by the age of twenty-nine. I also didn't care too deeply about my faith and if some tall, dark, and handsome upperclassman in the business department were to sweep me off my feet and take me with him to a school more prestigious than Hope while he pursued his master's degree in becoming The Man, I would have been completely okay with that.

Hope College is a unique Christian institution in that the participation of attending the chapel services and Sunday night events were always optional. The professors were versatile in terms of where they stood in their beliefs about God and I never felt like someone was throwing their dogmas in my face. This also made me more curious than ever. *Why weren't they throwing their dogmas in my face?*

The crazy thing about God is that when you make yourself available for Him to do something, more likely than not, He will. I learned this at Hope because, frankly, I was not there to seek Him. I simply made myself present and my heart was open to whatever was in store. I had always thought that hardcore Christians were the kind of people who would ceaselessly pest individuals like me about why they were right and I was wrong. But these people whom I became so familiar with on campus weren't attacking me at all. If anything, they didn't care what I believed. This was different than anything I had ever known. They were simply so in love the dude and were "hardcore" in a completely different way. The community I surrounded myself with lived their lives to exemplify His love that they kept claiming was existent and real, and they never really conveyed it by actually talking at me. I wasn't quite sure of what was going on most of the time, but if anything, this God character was seriously enticing.

Early on in my college career, I had the privilege of meeting Chris. Our campus wasn't the biggest property of land and it was very common to run into the same person at least three times per day. Chris, on the other hand, did this very intentionally with everyone. He always happened to be there for people exactly when they would need him—usually more than three times per day. I sometimes seriously questioned whether or not he had a hidden power of teleportation. As I would go about my class life and run into Chris on a routinely basis, he *always* had something new to share regarding what God did for him. It was as though he lived for sharing stories about God to as many people he could each day.

Once, I walked into the coffee shop where Chris worked and I could tell something was radiating from his heart. He grinned a huge grin as soon as he noticed me entering and came from behind the counter to take me by the shoulders to share a story. It was about how he had been praying to God about needing clarity on his future endeavors and God "spoke" to him through all of these different crazy avenues that led Chris to the answer he had been searching for.

I know that I am describing Chris to you as though he is nuts. But it's because he is. He was absolutely crazy about God. Obsessed is a better way to put it. But his obsession is undeniably captivating and I often found myself envious of what he had. What I didn't apprehend was *how* Chris would talk about his interactions with God. I understood that people around campus were usually advocates for the Christian lifestyle, but Chris didn't just live out a trend or force anything down my throat. He simply kept talking to me about God as if He was our next-door neighbor. And according to Chris, God seemed to be the wisest, overly caring, most generous and readily available next-door neighbor I had ever heard of.

***

Later in the same year, I was able to sit down with Chris during one of his breaks at the coffee shop and we naturally grabbed some coffee to go with our conversation. We talked about the weather and the weekend coming up ahead but it wasn't long before Chris mentioned God again. Without hesitance, I began to ask some questions.

"Chris, how do you spend time with God?"

"Oh, in many ways! I'm spending time with Him right now!"

"Well sure, okay. But I mean, how do you spend time with Him to build your *personal* relationship with him? Like, how do you get to know Him better? ...Am I making sense?" I had only asked because I wasn't even sure if I understood what I was inquiring.

Chris thoughtfully responded, "I pray, of course. Other than getting into the Word. I mean, I do find myself just sitting before His presence but that's usually when I have very little to say. This morning though I got up at five because I knew I wouldn't have had any other moment in the day to really give Him the quality time He deserves from me."

This conversation wasn't too long, mainly because Chris' break was up. But I walked away from that brief discussion feeling as though I had just spoken to a man who was head over heels with the love of his life. He talked about the Bible as though it was a collection of love letters from the most romantic soul and he went on about his times of prayer as if they were lively conversations with his favorite friend. I did not know much but I was confirmed of this: Chris had a *relationship* with God. He didn't just believe in Him, He *knew* Him. I had always noticed that Chris was one of those people who had an extra skip in his step, but I simply found that to be his personality. That was his personality and I was the type to be completely fine with not skipping at all if it meant I could preserve my energy. But no—there was something bigger going on; he was so in love. He didn't care what I thought or what anyone in Holland thought for that matter; he had a personal relationship with Jesus and he had to express in the way that anyone in love does.

***

I never really read the Bible or *The Word*, as Chris called it, outside from the times I had occasionally visited church. I didn't see the point. It was boring, outdated, and irrelevant. But again, I never read it all the way through either. I had no true case and point for my opinions. These were simply assumptions after years of solidifying due to the way Christians have misrepresented it to me.

I wanted to know what Chris was talking about. I had known him for a respectable period of time. He was not a foolish, nor was he unwise. He was one of the most down-to-earth people I had ever met who also happened to be all in it for this Jesus guy. I could hear all of my crazy intelligent atheist friends from high school laughing at me now, wondering when I had gone off the deep end and begun to turn into a Jesus freak. But Chris made me wonder what I had been failing to see all of these years. If someone who eats like me, talks like me, and is equally as bad as board games as me can communicate and connect with someone who was supposedly in complete control of life, why the heck would I choose to miss out on that? Maybe my poorly designed workout shirt from youth group was right; maybe I had only viewed Jesus to be a yet another religion thing and nothing more. I didn't know it to be a relationship. I didn't know how it could be.

Through that semester to the end of the school year, I committed to staying up two extra hours to read the Bible. If my past self had known that this was how I would be spending my nights at Hope College, she would have sent herself to the a top-ten party school instead to assure some fun (and sleep). But really, I needed to know the truth and I wanted to make sure I wasn't playing a fool with myself in this life that I had been given.

***

One of the most significant revelations I had while reading the Bible with a fresh set of eyes was that everything in the book had to be taken within context. Before, I had envisioned it to be a very thick set of instructions ordained by a judgmental and pompous god who was created by even more judgmental and pompous people. But in reality, it was a book full of history, dialogue, and poetry. There was no way one could just flip open this dense book and read a line and assume its law. It would have been just as silly as someone snatching this book from us and opening it to chapter three to automatically assume that all I care about is soup.

No. There is more to my life than soup, truth be told. There is more to the Bible than any one-liner we have ever heard.

If nothing else, this is what I neglected to hear all of the years: The Jesus story wasn't about some man coming and proclaiming what to do and what not to do in this world in a dramatic robe and untamed facial hair. It also wasn't just about people-swallowing fish or a bunch of unclothed people covered in leaves walking around in a garden. This was what I used to think the Bible was about. This was also why I thought Christians were nonsense.

But I had been mistaken.

I read it all and it told me something different.

The Bible is a story about a man who was God and *is* God. Now, let me stop myself before I go further and ask you, do you understand what that means? Imagine a man walking down the street just like how you and I would with regular shoes and a regular body. But because of His power of being able to control the universe, some mocked Him for thinking He could while others worshipped the very ground He walked on because He was God Himself. Which, in my opinion, makes sense why both would happen. I could see why this was a huge deal. But I could also easily see why it was hard to love Him right away. I didn't blame the nonbelievers in the Bible because they were simply trying to protect themselves from lies and false testimonies like we all do. No one likes to play the part of a fool. I could understand why many couldn't trust Him at all.

But listen, this man never needed to prove Himself but came down to earth anyway to show us that there surely is more to life than what we see here. There is more to life than money. There is more to life than these temporary highs. There is more to life than pain or trial. And there is certainly more to life than death.

This man's name is Jesus and He lived His life to exhibit exactly how selfless and loving our God in heaven is. He lived to show us the way to live the most fruitful kind of life so that one day when it is our time, we can be satisfied with our days past and forever spend eternity with Him in the place where we could go when we are no longer physically alive. The Bible isn't written to kill the joy of life; it is to attain it.

To gain our trust and understanding of God's love for humanity, Jesus took the most painful kind of death at the time and hung naked, bleeding on the cross for the world to see. This had to happen because so many did not believe what He had to say and they persecuted Him for it. In the meantime, the rest were too ashamed to stand up for Him. At this point in my reading, I kept questioning myself as to whether or not I would have had the courage to be on Jesus' side if I were to have lived in this moment of history. I don't know. I would like to say I would have. But in all fairness, it would have taken an awful lot of blind trust to believe in a man strutting around living like He was God himself. No wonder it is so difficult to believe in Him even in this time and age. No wonder humanity still keeps Jesus outside of so much of what engulfs us. It's easier to not care than to muster the strength to believe.

But here is the part that really got to me. Jesus didn't use His awesome powers to keep Himself from dangling vulnerably on the cross. That would have defeated the purpose of showing love in the first place. It would have been much like a rich dad buying his way into his children's hearts with his effortless money when he talked so much about how he would sacrifice everything he had. Jesus, in fact, did. He sacrificed Himself when He didn't have to. He became completely vulnerable and transparent out of His own will. But the story doesn't end there.

Thank God.

He rose again from the dead three days later with marks left on His body to identify what He had done for us. He undeniably proved His greatness and power by defeating death. This showed us that death has been conquered by Jesus and God Himself. It displayed to the world that we have nothing to fear as long as we are in a personal relationship with this man who was and *is* God. This relationship can sustain because He certainly is not dead, but eternally alive.

This is the gospel story, the greatest love story ever told. This is what the Bible was all about. This is what I discovered through that semester to the end of the school year. No one had actually sat me down and told it to me this way before. This kind of stuff was banned from my history books during grade school. And honestly, it wasn't anyone else's responsibility. It was mine. To hear about it is one thing, but to personally commit and testify that I believed it to be true was another. Even if someone tried to sway me with their convincing words and alluring strategies, something tells me that I still would not have believed like the way I did after reading the entire Bible for myself. It was always supposed to be my personal relationship with God and His son, Jesus. No one else could have set that up for me but He Himself with the works of the Holy Spirit.

Did I find many parts of the Bible difficult to believe? Oh heck yeah. Did I also feel outrageous at times to think all of what it said could be real? Of course! But this is the radical thing about choosing to be in a *relationship* with Jesus. The more you spend time reading what the Bible says, the clearer the message becomes. I wish I could explain it in a more sensible or logical way, but that's just it. It is beyond our senses and our logic. It is simply too good for words. Like skydiving into nothing or falling in love for the first time, it is an indescribable experience that we have to go try it for ourselves. Experiences like these also come with risks. But the rewards are far more satisfying than not trying at all. I will go as to say it is worth my life.

If we were to take a closer look at Jesus and call Him a friend, I definitely did not make a good friend back to Him in the past. I have had people gossip about Him to me and I have laughed about the lies for the sake of my own reputation. Imagine an old relative who you have created a distinct illusion for due to the fact that the only tangible things you knew about him or her were from the biased and skewed opinions of others. Like such, I have had false accusations about who Jesus was and what He did. I had heard awful rumors about His character and there was once a point when I believed them to be true. There had often been questioning of His sheer existence as well, but I never went to Him personally to consider the truth. This was all prior to knowing that it was supposed to be a relationship; I never cared to spend time with Him. When you don't put the work and effort into spending time with your friends, you don't really know them at all. It would come to a point where you wouldn't recognize them even if you were looking at them face to face.

The speaker from the women's leadership retreat from years ago was right. Like any relationship worth pursuing, we must place sacrificed time and work into building it. It's us who must make change to our hearts and attitudes about who Jesus was and is, not Him. He was and is always unconditionally there, waiting for us. And throughout this entire time, I had no idea that I secretly had personal fears and pains regarding what knowing God would be like. I think I had always envisioned Him to dislike who I had been and I was not ready for that kind of judgment or truth. But the Bible told me something different. He doesn't care about the past. He doesn't care at all as long as I knew that my identity was in Him. He carried all of the sins I had committed with Him and took my penalty for them on the cross. Regardless of my thickness and years of disbelief, here He was, captivating me with His irresistible love, taking me in and embracing who I was fully and relentlessly.

***

I don't ever want to walk right past Jesus in my life again. I want to know that when I see Him, I know His face well and that I find His voice to be familiar. I want to know that I could walk around with my eyes closed and sense His closeness because that is how well I know my friend, my Savior, my God.

And how, exactly, do I spend time with Him now? I spent time alone. By this, I mean I spend my time alone with God;

the One who Jesus came down to earth to embody. He is everywhere. He is where ever we find ourselves. Spending time alone is literally my favorite thing to do in this world. This statement is truly outstanding because those who know me well would tell you that I am not someone who comes off as a girl who would enjoy time away from other people. I love people and I relish the livelihood of others. But I would choose my alone time with God over anything. It really is my favorite thing. This is when I can hear my echoed prayers. This is when I feel the closest to home.

Some people go further in their relationship with Him by writing love songs or singing praises, but I like to go on trips. Much like my time spent with Jane, I like to go on bike rides, long runs, or spontaneous road trips by myself for a while to get to know God and for me to be real before Him. I like to sit in the passenger's seat while He takes the wheel and tells me about why He is guiding me in the way that He does. It gives me room to reflect and to make a point to understand who I was, who I am now, and who I aim to be. Amongst chaos and noise when surrounded with others in this world, it can be difficult to reflect. I love spending time with God and God alone because it is ultimately the way I find myself peacefully whole again.

***

There is only one place in the world where I order the exact same food every time I go in. I am usually an advocate for broadening horizons. However, at the City Delicatessen located right across the street from where Chris worked, I always find myself ordering what was called *The Denver*. It was originally a sporadic decision when I entered the restaurant during their grand opening. I went with it because I was a fan of Colorado and I didn't care to read through every detail of each sandwich listed on the menu.

Recently when I ordered my regular meal at the City Deli, my server and I had a pretty entertaining conversation. She had recognized me from all of the previous times and cared to make a mild observation.

"You're all about the guac, aren'tcha?" she stated as she was ringing me up.

"Excuse me?"

"*The Denver* is one of our only options with guacamole. That is why you order it every time, isn't it?"

It may sound ridiculous, but I seriously had no idea that that's what I was eating. I simply ordered a sandwich that I became very fond of and after a while, I never found it important to question the content within the deliciously golden baguette.

"I'm eating *guacamole*?"

My server stared at me, trying not to make a judgment, "Yeah, yeah you are. I think you kinda love it."

"Isn't guacamole made from avocados? I don't like avocados."

"Have you tried it before?"

"Well, no. I 'spose I haven't. But I didn't think I'd ever want to."

"Well you are obviously all about it! You just didn't know it yet!"

I nodded and smiled as I took yet another Denver-to-go. I stepped out of those doors feeling quite silly and mystified. I was mystified because it made me laugh out loud at how little I knew of what I actually liked and disliked. There were aspects of my life I adopted on a regular basis and never took the time to give appreciation in its rightful place. This was because I simply took things for what they were and nothing more. Apparently I am all about avocados. I rely on its goodness every time I walk into the City Deli.

Much like this uncompromising reality, I believe this is how I had been with the concept of God in the past. I never thought I liked Him, nor did I desire to give Him a try. But I had lived my life in such a way where He had been keeping accounts on me all along. Regardless of my knowledge in my desire for Him, He was always present. I simply took His goodness in my past to be pure luck or a coincidence. I had no idea I was tasting His sheer brilliance along the way. I had no idea I was relying on Him but dismissing His presence the entire time.

I now think about God now every time I see avocados. Whether it is in the supermarket, on the television, in salads or even on Taco Bell's menu, I notice it all around and I always think about God. I think about how I should never underestimate the given things in life nor dismiss what a marvel He is. I think about how He comes in various forms and I should never be too surprised if I find Him in the most peculiar places. I also think about God when I see avocados because it is a little inside joke between Him and me. If I know anything about good relationships worth keeping, it is that they have many inside jokes and it's okay if no one else gets it. That's why they're personal. My relationship with God is personal and hilarious. I think I will always like avocados because they mean something so special to me that others won't understand. And I am completely okay with it.

Chapter Seven:
Something About Eternity

When I was sixteen, I picked up work at a Cold Stone Creamery within walking distance from my high school. If you have never stepped into a Cold Stone Creamery before, that's really okay. I will not be the one to encourage you. To purchase an overpriced dessert that carries enough calories to suffice for dinner is personally outrageous. However, it is quite the experience and an offer to take up if a friend is willing to pay.

Everyday (along with sporadic episodes of impromptu singing), we were to restock the mix-in jars. They were the containers on the front line of the counter that displayed to the customers what candies and fruits were available to toss into their ice cream. Not only did they need to consistently be three-quarters full, but they also needed to be aesthetically pleasing. It was always about the aesthetics.

"Ughhh~ this is the *worst*," Brian would say. Brian was my shift manager and I would find him repeating this toward a new thing in the backroom every given hour. Arms flailing and all. He was also one of the most outspoken drama kings I had ever met.

I enjoyed choosing shifts within Brian's agenda because I secretly found his theatrical energy to be entertaining and life-giving. However, it always took me a little while to gather my patience to truly empathize with my twenty-year-old supervisor as he equated life-threatening diseases with pimples or a new girl in town.

"Ji," Brian exclaimed one day, "Look at me; this is serious talk."

"Yeah Brian?"

"This is the absolute worst!"

This time, he was restocking the jar of Reese's peanut butter cups. Immediately I felt pity for Brian. All the workers from earlier shifts had left that jar undone because it really was "the worst". The task was extra tedious because one had to unpack a giant cardboard box of Reese's peanut butter cups from the depths of the freezer, take out all the smaller boxes from the larger box, and within those boxes were infinite amounts of individually wrapped Reese's peanut butter cups which then one would have to neatly and carefully unwrap and stack with precision and thought into the mix-in jar. It was also important to handle these maneuvers keenly and swiftly so the chocolate would not melt. The whole project really was a hands-on SAT test, scoring specifically on geometry and physics.

"In *my* hell, this is all anyone would ever be doing. Forever."

I laughed. We both laughed. And as the giggling dwindled, we laughed some more. *What a silly idea*, I thought. I gave him a final smirk as I went about mopping, then I actually pondered upon what he said. Brian wasn't a believer of God, or at least from what I could tell. We would play songs in the backroom with cuss words in it and he would always enlighten me about his crazy weekend parties with colorful verbs. But he thought about hell, apparently.

I had never really thought deeply about hell. For me, it was a door in my mind that I had placed a thick roll of caution tape in front of ever since I read about destruction and death in the Bible. I never actually had gotten to the point to freak out and block the doorway with the strips of tape. But it was a place I purposely ignored.

I had been told throughout the years that one couldn't fathom places like heaven and hell. They were far beyond our senses, they would be described as hyper-reality; far beyond all that our brains could attain from this world. But I wanted to know what to do with that roll of caution tape I had left in front of my hell door from who-knows-when. If I were to allow myself to have thoughts, opinions, and ideas about these scary places called heaven and hell, I needed to start somewhere. And the only 'somewhere'-s I knew were of this world. This world is the only realm I had ever been. And yet, I felt like a wannabe hippie or a priest every time my mind drifted off into existential ideas like this. I was stuck between curiosity and indifference. It was not until the death of a friend two years down the road where God really hit me with the truth that thinking about the life beyond death mattered.

***

It was a Saturday when I received the phone call that Ryan had committed suicide. It was partly cloudy and I remember random things about the day. For example, I was wearing a mint green sweater and I had spilled homemade salsa on the left sleeve. I was also hosting a birthday party later in the evening and on the following Monday I had a paper due which already had my stress-meter spinning wild. But what was this thought and talk of stress in a moment so uncalled for as Ryan's death?

Stress and anxiety does not even begin to put into words the turmoil one experiences when a person so near to the heart passes away. As irrational as it may seem, I remember still attending all of my duties and walking through the movements on autopilot that night. I did not speak of Ryan, nor did I show it on my face.

I did not tell anyone that day about Ryan or the fact that I was dying inside because I did not even know how I would react. It wasn't simply the courtesy of not ruining someone else's day; it was about me. I did not know it at the time, but my course of decisions was guided by my very selfish intentions that day. They were cautionary acts to inhibit myself from being real because reality was too bitter to swallow and I was too prideful to admit this.

Ironically, I was working for Hope College's Campus Ministries office at the time. I was running several errands for the upcoming week and it had been thirty hours since I had been notified of Ryan. It had been thirty hours since I had lost a friend here on earth and it already felt like an eternity in my world.

The concept of time is such a fascinating and funny tool. We live in our days and count our twenty-four hours within our seven-day week when in reality, we are actually living in someone's highly functional and innovative idea of astronomy and division while eternity is spinning before us. Time in itself is an ambiguous matter and we disregard the potential being that we are tasting the slightest glimpses of eternity as we speak. Although we don't get it all, I believe we are able to attain very minimized but vivid realities of what eternity in heaven or hell could seem. Because when you're sulking in grievance and the blunt truth of someone's unpredicted death, there is no timeframe to attain such a circumstance. I entered the Campus Ministries office around eight in the evening and in the blink of an eye, I caught myself still standing there with two minutes 'til ten. You feel as though the world should cut its horseplay and stop mocking you for just a little while until you have mustered the strength to count the twenty-four hours within the seven days again.

Finding my numb body stationed in the dark lobby of the office, I wondered when my feet would hurry out of there before eternity caught me drifting again. I took on a new definition of hellish and freaked myself out. There, then, I looked across the room and there stood a wooden cross leaning against the wall. If there was, indeed, a Father in heaven, He was never really near. I could not see his face. I could only see his knees and his ankles. His black socks.

He spoke cheap things like, "Ji, no. It's okay. It's alright. I'm here. Look. Come to me!"

Scornfully, I looked upon that wooden cross,

"No. You are not."

***

I remember thinking hard about Ryan that night. I'll be honest, I wondered if he was going to hell. I mean, what is that process anyway? Does the whole world wait until the human population dies off and then our souls merrily skip to our separate ways of eternity? Or is it all happening right now? Are there twenty-four hours within a seven-day week in these eternal places? They say hell is the worst thing we could possibly imagine. That's the only tangible way it can really be described because the truth is that it is actually intangible and very much beyond what we can imagine. Did Ryan suffer here on earth only to suffer more in a place so unspeakable? Is Ryan suffering right now when I could have done something to stop it all?

I would have rather not thought about this. Throwing God out the window and choosing to believe that we simply become one with the dirt again was a much more pleasant idea. That way I didn't have to know whether or not the people I loved were or weren't the ones our Almighty God had in mind for His exclusive place called heaven.

I didn't know why I survived the battle of suicide and Ryan did not. *That's not fair, God.* I didn't understand why we had to experience this kind of pain in this world. In this time of grief and turmoil, I almost felt like I was already in hell. I wasn't sure if Ryan was there but I felt like I certainly was. Thinking about it all was killing me and to not think about it killed me, too.

***

God sent me an angel in the form of a stranger on the street that night. I was walking home and it was roughly three in the morning. I was dragging my feet in the most annoying way and I did it to see if I even cared. Looking back, the whole thing really could have been a melodramatic scene in some black and white film from the seventies. I kept my head facing straight forward but my eyes were clouded with dry tears and confusion. My vision was such a haze that I failed to notice a man in a wheelchair coming toward me. When I finally saw that the murky figure ahead was not a random bush growing straight out of the sidewalk but was a man, I literally let out a yelp. Immediately I felt apologetic because I felt like it was offensive.

As I kept walking, I couldn't help but slow down when I neared him. Something seemed to be wrong with his wheelchair. He was tilted and I peered down to see that the tire on one of his smaller wheels was practically off of the frame.

"You look like you want to help me," the man said.

Startled again, I flinched a little and looked his face. Much of his features were hidden amongst the shadows of the night but the tone of his voice was both inviting and soft.

"Yes, yes I do," I groggily replied, "How can I be of help?"

"Well, I don't know," the man said, "My chair's been bent like this ever since I can remember. It always takes a while for me to get anywhere. Today's been hard though. Harder than usual."

I wished to know why he was out so late. But it seemed out of place to ask. I bent down and tried to slip the worn tire back onto the frame of the wheel and to my dismay, it was much more difficult than I had predicted. In fact, it seemed like I could do absolutely nothing about it. He wasn't kidding when he said it's been like that forever.

"I'm sorry, sir. I'm really trying."

"It's okay. I appreciate that you're even taking the time, really."

As I found myself at eye level with the man, I smiled at him and he smiled back. I could see his face a little better. What he gave back was something so kind and genuine.

"Thank you for doing what you could," he said, "That's good enough."

"Oh, but I can do so much better. Let me try again."

He moved away his wheelchair, "No. I promise. That is good. And that is enough. I mean it in the best way. You can let go now."

So I did. I let go. And he began to maneuver himself away.

Before he moved too far, he turned his head around and spoke these simple words to me, "It's going to be okay. It always is. You can go home now. You can rest. Let it be. Let me be."

I didn't know why he said it like that. And I didn't know why I received it in the way that I did. But I was no longer thinking about his wheelchair. And maybe the following happened because I was so fixated on the loss of Ryan but if I didn't know any better, this man slowly moving away from me had such familiar eyes...eyes that reminded me of Ryan's. I felt like I was watching Ryan and he was telling me to let it go and to get it right with God. I felt like he was looking at me with an eternal affirmation that it was going to be okay; it already is. I stopped dragging my feet. And, indeed, I went home, just like the man told me to. I went home and I let it be. I let him be. By the grace of God, my heart was beating easily again by the time I reached my dorm. I could breathe a little better as I closed my eyes to sleep.

"That is good. And that is enough," I kept repeating to myself as I drifted away, "That is good. And that is enough."

***

The thing is, I will never really know until I am there. Any of it. The truth about eternity. The truth about Ryan. The truth about life. And the truth about death. I don't know if I will see Ryan again. I hope so. I really do. I pray about it and I pray with a hopeful spirit. Like everything else in life, we can choose to believe all we want on the realties of experiencing something. But we have no authority to personally claim that we know what life beyond what is here on earth looks like until we find ourselves there.

But listen; here is what I do know. There are other people all around us who are struggling. There are also people all around who have no idea that they are struggling at all. There are over 150,000 deaths occurring in this world every day. Death is nothing uncommon, yet in those raw moments when you see how intense the brink of death is, you realize that a life is a life. No one's is more significant than another's. But no one's is less crucial either. There are eternal joys and eternal pains that are being solidified as these seconds pass on by and we still have chances to be present in someone else's life before their physical death.

***

Maybe the Bible is really getting at something when it says that we ought to live each day as if it were the last...because for my dear friend Ryan, it was. And for me on that dreaded night before the homecoming dance, it easily could have been. It may not be the last day for you but it could be for your waitress, your teacher, your sister, or your best friend. Maybe the best way to focus on eternity is to focus on the present. To cherish everything here in the moment so that the burden of knowing you could have made an extra phone call or notice something was going wrong before it's too late doesn't have to exist. We can be a part of straightening those front wheels in one another's lives before they become something undeniably permanent and unfixable. It's never our responsibility to rectify, but is it not an absolute joy to know that we get a chance to be a part of someone's reason to keep living?

Maybe the key to understanding heaven and hell is to be so keen and aware of the daily happenings that are laced with hints of eternity. Maybe this will help us differentiate when someone is just being quiet to when someone dying inside. And maybe we can notice that as much as there are people loving life, there are people around us living in hell and no one is taking the time to meet them where they're at. Maybe this is how we can play a part in their eternity. Maybe we can try to reflect what this place called heaven will look like for those around us so that we are certain we did our best. So that we don't find ourselves unmovable in the darkness of an office lobby neck-deep in guilt and self-doubt.

Perhaps it is true that heaven is a place we cannot approach with sufficient words or images, but what if we are able to make room for more opportunities for the ones around us to have a taste of what that would look like? Because when we taste something so good, we only crave more of it. But unlike anything here on earth, we won't get sick off of too much. We can only drown in the glory of it...the kind of drowning where it is helpless but desired from the heart. For the first time in our lives, we are willing to completely let go because we are blindly confident that it is right. And for all the times we have shouted out loud, "I wish I could live forever like this!" Maybe we can. Maybe we will. Those are the shards of truth that hints to our hearts where our soul longs to find itself at the end of time.

***

Perhaps there is a purpose to it all. Maybe the things we do here on a daily basis does matter. Like the way we a ripple expands from the smallest collisions of the surface of tranquil waters. Maybe this is why we should take more chances. Because we might just be someone's only chance in that given day. We might just be a miraculous phone call for a guy like Ryan. You might just be a miraculous phone call for me, and I, you.

I hope my old manager Brian doesn't have to peel back the wretched wrappings of his Reese's peanut butter cups for eternity. I hope that no one on my watch becomes a slave to his or her miseries. I hope he will be dancing in heaven with me. I hope we can give each other high fives in our favorite tacky Cold Stone Creamery costumes and rejoice at the fact that it wasn't about whether we were right or wrong, it was about the fact that we got there. It wasn't about us, it was about the glory of God, and it wasn't about the things we had left undone, it was about the fact that it is finished.

Chapter Eight:
Love Because

ere's a confession: I never did laundry growing up.

I can hear all of the eyes rolling within the sockets now. *What a spoiled child, Ji was*...I know, I hear you. But listen, I never had to. This was the one thing my mother relentlessly insisted on doing for me until the day I moved out. Now that I think about it, I hardly even remember her actually doing it in front of me. She was like a laundry ninja. One minute my clothes were dirty and the next thing I knew, they were back into my drawers smelling like flowers from some distant, mystical land of pink fragrances. Most of the time she was not even present in the house. She really was a ninja about the whole concept.

For a while I shrugged this off as yet another symptom of her extreme type-A personality, but there was something more. Although verbal affirmation was rare in the house, my mother always did my laundry. This was her way of loving me. I don't think I was aware of this at the time. I think many of us usually are not so perceptive on love when it is served to us in these creative avenues. But in retrospect, my mother faithfully did love me everyday, especially on those days after the muddy track workouts.

I find everything about love to be truly comical and tragic. There are so many mediums in which love accesses and utilizes, but more often than not, these seemingly valid and thoughtful acts of love go unnoticed. It is not so much the fault of the lover or the beloved, but rather the lack of communication as a whole.

For me, to understand the love of Jesus took an extensive amount of time because there was a huge lack of understanding how He communicated with me. I remember sitting around my bed late at night and taking strolls alone in the park hoping that this Jesus guy would soon come and bring my soul to life, whatever that meant. Then perhaps confestti would wondrously fall from the sky and my world would be figured out because the presence of life's ultimate definition of love was before me. I didn't really know how to receive His love, let alone seek it.

***

In high school, I used to fret about what love was supposed to be like. Anyone who claimed they were in love said they could not describe it, which made it difficult to believe whether they had the real thing or not. While the movies made it seem as though it could only be felt if we were in Paris or had script in our hands with poetry about birds or something borderline barf-worthy like that. Yet I could not get it off my radar because every time love was mentioned, it seemed to do pretty crazy and mind-blowing things for people. For a while I wanted it to be just a psychological thing. Or maybe a hormonal thing of being human and bored all at the same time. But all of these individuals who have married and fallen madly and passionately in this notion of love could not have gotten together one day while I wasn't looking and make it up just to play me like a fool. If they did, I think I would be weirdly flattered. It was something real that we seemed to be able to experience and feel, like an aroma or a warmth. But this belief did not lessen my anxiety about it. I still felt like there should have been a mathematical equation or a book for dummies about it.

This concern about understanding love hit me hard when my lockermates (yes, I shared my four-foot tall locker with multiple girls who had multiple make-up bags for gym class) both found boyfriends and hung their favorite athletic photos of them in their portion of the locker space. It was not envy that I experienced during this season, but rather bewilderment. As far as I could tell, the girls in my class had been on the constant prowl since we first began our reproductive health courses with Mr. Gebben eons ago while I was that incessant friend who tried to play the wise guy by asking stupid questions like, "are you sure you're ready for a relationship?" and, "how do you know he is *the one*?" I just didn't understand. I didn't get how people could take something so uncertain and run so confident in it.

During the same year, I was taking chemistry (ironically) for my last period and it was taught in the green hall. I recall feeling pretty special because most of the students in the classroom were a year above me. This was kind of a big deal in our high school. I thought this meant that I was a genius. In reality, it meant that I had bit off more than I could chew yet again and my GPA was going to surface as mediocrely as the girl's sitting in front of me.

Speaking of the girl sitting in front of me, she never seemed to be fully there, if you get what I mean. I would stare at the back of her strawberry blonde head and watch it move back and forth while I imagined it to be like a pendulum keeping a steady pace for the seconds of school to shave off in a painfully slow manner. She was also always doodling and writing in her notebook. For a little while I assumed she was taking notes, but I was wrong. She would write even when our teacher would stop speaking. I would find her writing during that awkward time when we would wait for that last kid to hand in the three-question pop quiz. Not to mention also the last five minutes of everyday while everyone else was anticipating for the ringing of the bell. She would still be sitting at her lab desk, writing until the very last second.

The day after spring break, our teacher found it to be a brilliant idea to switch our seating arrangements. He said something about how we were becoming nullified and no one really knew what that meant. I was rearranged next to Strawberry Blonde and I used this chance to investigate what I had been so curious about.

"What are you always writing?" I asked on a Tuesday while we were working on ways to create molecular structures with mini marshmallows and toothpicks. She looked at me puzzled and a little bit dazed. I helped by pointing my pinky finger at her purple Mead notepad sitting beneath the bag of marshmallows.

She timidly smirked and took a moment to speak. For a minute I thought she was going to make up a lie because the smirk on her face wasn't out of humor, it was from being surprisingly exposed.

"They're letters."

"Oh?"

"Yeah. They're letters to my future husband."

I'm ninety-nine percent sure that my face told all that my brain was thinking. I didn't mean to. It just kind of happened. I looked at my lab partner with an expression people make when they hear a fart and want to be courteous by obliviously pretending they had lost the sense of smell. She was bold enough to go on to say that she would care to explain it fully to me if I was willing to listen. Surprisingly enough, I took her up on the offer and I found myself spending the night at her house the following weekend.

So, there we were on an air mattress in the middle of her parent's family room with boxes of Mike-and-Ike's and a family-size bag of Twizzlers. Strawberry Blonde told me that she had recently read a book on love and it had changed her life. She said she was done with the concept of dating and having crushes on boys our age. Until the man of her dreams came stumbling in and she knew it was the right time, she had this profound plan of writing to the special guy everyday so that he would know when they met that she had been loyal to him all along.

Personally, whenever I heard anyone use the term *man* around me, it made me squirm. Maybe I was immature but it grossed me out a little. I didn't want to think about men. Or their beards.

"Wow. Well, that's love," I said unsophisticatedly because I needed some genuine way to respond. Truth is, I had no idea if that was love. It sounded kind of outlandish to me. Then again, I was also still caught up with this idea that everyone took a prerequisite course on love before they entered high school and I missed the sign-up sheets when they were going around.

She could sense my uncertainty and spoke with a reassuring and an almost overconfident voice, "it's not that I am against dating or anything, Ji. People can do that. That's fine. I just see now that it's a very underclassmen-like thing to do."

I tried not to take that comment too offensively.

She went on, "Dating is just what people busy themselves with until true love actually comes knocking on the door. It explains it all in the book. Like, all of my friends right now are wasting their efforts dating random boys on the varsity hockey team."

A few of the guys on the varsity hockey team were friends of mine. I tried envisioning any of my guy friends being *the one* for someone. It made me chuckle but I refrained to show it for the sake of better judgment within a seemingly stern conversation.

She continued, "I feel sorry for all of my girls because I know they're filling empty space. They're dating the hockey guys right now because being patient for the right one is hard. But like my softball coach says, nothing worth having in life comes easy. I think it's worth it to be patient for love, and it obviously doesn't happen in high school."

I felt like we were in a talk show and it was at the part when the audience is told to applaud regardless of whether or not they were paying attention or even found it necessary. I respected her for being so open and honest about a seemingly deep topic, especially for a Friday night while sitting upon a leaky air mattress. However, I couldn't help but detect several holes in her philosophy of a perfect and selective love.

"Are you allowed to love other people in between?" I asked.

"What do you mean?"

"Like, are you allowed to share a little bit of your love to the people who come and go in your life until you know you have met the right one?"

"Oh, I see," she responded as she took a confident bite out of her Twizzler, "My answer would be...no. I think that takes away the whole purpose. I am doing this to save myself up so I don't exert energy on pointless relationships."

"What about your mom?"

"What about my mom?"

"Well, don't you have to save some love for her?"

"Oh my gosh, Ji. That's so different."

"How so?"

"It just is."

With no more words, we both bit into our Twizzlers at the same time and hit our weary heads unto our pillows. She asked if I wanted to keep one of the lamps on while we slept and I said sure. As we quickly drifted away into our separate dreams, it dawned on me that we never did brush our teeth that night.

***

Needless to say, she went on to study finance in college and is to this day one of the finest investors I know. She saves everything she comes in contact with like a boss and is more knowledgeable about budgeting than I will ever be.

But as far as love went, I wasn't quite sure if it was something we were supposed to keep tucked away. I wasn't sure if it was something we budget and organize in these cabinets set so rigidly in our minds. I still had questions lingering from that Friday night and I had a feeling they could not be answered by people my own age.

***

I think although the concept of love is known to be certainly grand and powerful, some of us fail to see it because of a disconnect. Whether we don't get the definition right in our heads or we find our hearts misplaced in this world, it can become tragically unfamiliar to us. It is not to say that love never existed in the picture, but rather that somewhere in the transaction, it isn't exposed in such a way for it to truly reach, change, and potentially save another's life. It is produced without the need of guarantees from the start, like a football that is never be promised to make it to touchdown. To better explain why I began to see it this way, I want to share a story about a woman named Anne.

During spring break of my sophomore year in college, a few buddies and I went down to Newark, New Jersey on a mission trip to help serve in the urban school systems. Newark had been ranked numerous times to be one of the nation's poorest cities and this journey truly was an eye-opening experience for us all. Mission trips are a funny thing because our original intent is to go and help the world out there in one way or another. But most often than not, we will come back realizing that the world actually did us a favor. If executed well, we would return home with some new perspective. The hope, then, would be that we'd go back one day to actually make a difference. My experience with Newark definitely taught me something great, but it was not what I thought I was in for.

While there, I met a woman by the name of Anne. She was from the same the neighborhood where we were located. Anne and other older women from the area generously made brunch for us on one of the Sundays during our visit. Many people from the community had gathered and it truly was a beautiful scene. Toward the end of the meal, I quietly excused myself from the table to find the restroom within the building's small corridors, and mistakenly, I stepped into an office space where Anne was standing in the middle with her back facing the doorway.

"I'm sorry, Anne!" I exclaimed, "I didn't mean to interrupt."

"Oh! That's fine, dear," Anne gently replied. Her voice was solemn and her movements were soft. As she turned around to acknowledge me, I noticed she was holding a photo in her hand.

I could not view the image from where I stood but whatever it was, Anne seemed pretty upset about it. I peered around to see that no one else was around and took a moment to measure if it was appropriate for me to approach her.

"Are you okay?" I carefully asked. I stepped toward Anne as the sound of my heels clicking on the old wooden floor announced my rather overbearing entrance.

Anne's face grew into a deep smile as she looked me in the eyes to confirm all is well. She had a sweet, earnest essence about her. There didn't seem to be a hurry for anything with Anne. When I was around her, it felt easy.

As I politely smiled back, Anne lifted up the photograph for me to see. She then began to tell me why this was a day for mourning.

The photo was of her three grandchildren; two handsome boys and one little girl. In her slow and patient manner, Anne explained to me how the father of these three children passed away several years back of a heart attack. He also happened to be her son. She was sad because their mother, also her daughter-in-law, never really warmed up to her and therefore moved away soon after the father's death and neglected to inform Anne on her or her children's whereabouts.

This day marked yet another anniversary of the passing of her son and yet another year of Anne not knowing where her beloved grandchildren resided.

As I listened, I could feel the waves of Anne's timidly shaking voice. My heart shook with hers and for a moment I wished I were God so I pluck the children from where they were with giant tweezers and place them right there in this room with us. I felt Anne's deep and desperate cry and I so badly wished I could do something to help.

I took another glance at the photo that was in her pale, slender hands. Her grandchildren really were beautiful. The little girl was about three when the picture was taken and she had Anne's cheekbones, spunk to her posture, and an indescribable radiance.

"I would run to where ever they're at," Anne stammered.

Anne was a woman nearing her sixties. For her to declare that she would run anywhere at all was quite the statement in itself. I stared at her in a way where I wanted to soak up every ounce of emotion I could sense overflowing from her pores. She kept her face real close to mine and it was almost as though my proximity assured her I was both physically and sentimentally with her.

"I'm sure they miss you."

"I just love them so very much, you hear?"

"You know, Anne, I have a feeling they've always known, too."

"Well I hope so, Ji. I pray to God for them every mornin' before I find myself busy with anything else in the day. It's why I do what I do here. These grandkids of mine are the reason I won't move from this city, as horrendous as it is getting. Don't get me wrong, I do enjoy the people and all, but I have dreams too, you see. I could be gone doin' other stuff. But these kids are my everything. They're the only dream I can see right now. So I's stays here in case they come lookin' for me! I pray about it everyday. I just won't let it go."

This, if I was not mistaken, was love.

Unconditional, unfathomable, unbeatable love.

***

One of the key topics we focused on during our mission trip was the discipline of perseverance. We had to persevere through the long days and endure within the trials that came with serving in such unfamiliar territories. We needed to study the definition well and practice its attributes with the way we carried ourselves. While on the topic of perseverance, we also dove into discussions about how we could most certainly use this virtue in the ways we love.

As I sat in these conversations and often led them, I had Anne and her three grandchildren on the forefront of my mind. When I took the time to truly unravel the fervor and zeal that Anne had for the children within the photo she kept close to her heart, I could not help but imagine that this was how Jesus loved us and how He loves us still. I would think about Anne and how she boldly declared that she would *run* to where her grandchildren were to meet them there. I pictured Jesus running after us, chasing with undeniable love and passion dialed in His eyes, regardless of our posture. I envisioned the world trying so hard to take us away from the love that is Jesus, much like the way Anne's daughter-in-law took a hold of these grandchildren's lives and escorted them to some place so distant from Anne. But much like Jesus and His unconditional character, it didn't matter Anne's circumstance or agenda. She had urgency that persevered for these kids whom she knew by their individual names and very intentionally lived her life for. They were the first things she spoke from her lips the moment she awoke and the last things on her heart before she went to bed. And something told me that her dreams had between the night to the morning were nothing different.

Although these kids might not have the slightest clue, they still have someone to this day who protects them with words of prayer and an ever-loving heart. They are so dearly loved. They have been since they were born. If only they knew.

I also believe we have someone doing this for us as well. I believe we have had Him and His protection and love since the day we were born. If only we knew. To love is to be able to lay one's life down for another. To love is to be like Jesus for one another. To love is to know God. God, then, is love.

I began to understand. I began to stop questioning.

***

I think it is very easy for us to become distant with Jesus because of the inevitable fact that the last time He physically showed up on earth was approximately two thousand years ago. It isn't hard to detach ourselves with what He did for us on the cross because it no longer seems relevant to our everyday lives. Like the way Anne's grandchildren probably walk around nonchalantly and with very little idea the grief and sorrow their biological and physically distant grandmother feels for them on a daily basis, we also take our breaths for granted here on earth and not knowing we are desperately desired, loved, and protected by an awesome and ever-present God in heaven. I think we sometimes forget about the incredibly significant meaning behind why Jesus made a point to come into our lives in the first place years and years ago. We make a very relevant thing irrelevant for the sake of our laziness and convenience. We make Him an option when He constantly makes us His priority.

In my opinion, the most radical reality about His love is that we have access to the truth whenever we want. Whether or not we choose to accept His love or believe that He is with us and for us, it does not alter the certainty that He is still very much present and that His love will still exist. This goes against so much of what we know of this world. This is true love and because it is rare, we now have all sorts of distorted meaning of what love really is. The truth to life's core is often found waiting and persevering with hopeful expectancy to be discovered. Much like the way Anne's love extends from where she stands, it's not Jesus' fault if we personally decide to live within boundaries that keep us from hearing His heart.

***

Love isn't defined by the deed of kissing, cuddling, or seducing with a sexy outfit. It is not even simply the act of spending years together to make it mean something or the numerous letters written to prove a point. It is not a set of hoops carefully aligned to jump through, or a concept that can be held in a book for dummies like I had once hoped for. These are simply the gestures and memories we attach ourselves to with while our human hearts cling and mistake them for love. We try to save room in our heart for this pseudo definition of love because this takes work that wears us out. But if it was real love—the kind of love that Jesus exposed—it wouldn't tire us; it would revive us.

Maybe we're supposed to love freely. Perhaps we are supposed to love as often as we can and to save it is to limit it. Maybe what Strawberry Blonde was talking about was intimacy and romance, but love in its very definition extends so much more than that. As far as the meaning of love goes, it is universal and abundant.

Love, in its purest and finest form, is the self-sacrifice to serve willfully and to accept unconditionally. Love isn't simply closed off for our sizzling hot relationships or the affection one has with his or her mother. We don't need to prove something as deep as love, nor should we need to. It ought to be worn. Love is who we are from the inside out because it is embedded within us and it is what we constantly aim to become. Love is a limitless verb that is shown and given freely without the boundaries of circumstance or reason. To love is to be like Jesus. And He loved everyone. I have come to believe that the most authentic and indisputable way we can give ourselves to one another with love is by doing it without any set of expectations or bargains, rules or wages, even if it means we lose a lot. To offer one another love and grace is to do it out of an unconditional heart. Otherwise it isn't love and grace. It's just a few goofy photos hanging inside of a locker and everyone doing their own laundry all the time. Don't just love because you know you'll get love back. Love because.

Chapter Nine:

Bob

Enrolling at a private university was never on my radar, especially one that was small, liberal arts, and shamelessly Christian. As far as I was concerned, these institutions were the most irrational way to achieve a college degree. I didn't understand why someone would pay three or four times more than the usual tuition bill so that they could receive a bachelor's degree from some school no one knew about and the only memorable thing was that their roommate claimed to be the president's niece so you could glean the free sweatshirts from her.

Neither my mother nor my stepfather received education past high school due to economic circumstances growing up and as their oldest child, I felt the weight of responsibility to play out every endeavor they could not achieve for themselves. When it came to choosing colleges, I had a few things in mind. And when I say "a few things", I really mean that they all funneled back down to one main objective: *How far is it and how little can I visit home?* I so badly thirsted for acceptance and approval and this was the time to find it. I think my mother knew it, too. As much as it is every mother's fear that her child will never return, she also couldn't bear to tell me that she would miss me. So I didn't either. She kept pushing the top schools of the Midwest while I sought out schools at least nine hours of a drive away.

As I began to receive the acceptance letters from institutions from a nine-hour-radius and all else in between, I also happened to receive a brochure from a place called Hope College in the mail. I remember taking an easy glance at it and noticing an invitation for a visit. It came with a free meal. Knowing well that I wouldn't attend but also knowing well that free meals did not come by often, I decided to go to this visitation day on a whim and it was the best accident God has ever led me to make.

***

It was a chapel day when I visited Hope and although I could not tell you who was speaking or what the message was about, the experience was astonishing. The place was so crowded and I was told that the students were all there out of a personal choice. People were openly transparent in their thoughts and voices and the atmosphere grabbed me.

Then, I was able to visit the art building. I felt so empowered to etch this into my schedule. I knew that stepping inside such a place would have broke my parents' hearts, but I needed to. I wanted to see how my soul would react. I had been informed that it would simply "feel right" when I stepped foot onto the college I belonged in. I thought this was past me. But the moment I walked into the art studios, it felt right. I loved it. This was it. Hope College had what I wanted and it allowed me to break free again. I was meant to create and I secretly always knew it. It allowed me to breathe in the way I was meant to. I thought back to every time I had been scolded for doodling when I was supposed to be doing math. I was good at the other things, but I didn't love them. I didn't love math. I didn't love science. I loved art. I also loved these people who were able to express themselves, I loved Hope's art building, and I loved the idea of not knowing what was going to happen.

***

I lied to my parents that year. I told them I was rejected from all of the schools they wanted me to attend. I told them I had no choice but to attend Hope College, which was a tiny little school humorously only a hop, skip, and a jump away. They laughed and said I must be joking. And when I told them I wasn't, they were petrified. This was when I saw the worst of my parents. This was also when I stopped calling home, even amongst the various financial and health concerns going on. I left for college and I hardly made a point to return.

***

The first semester was a bit of a reality check for me. Aside from the trauma of thinking my mother could potentially pass away every other day, I still wasn't quite sure what I was doing in Holland, Michigan, with this spiteful desire to become a creative prodigy of a sort. I was enrolled in a handful of art courses and I quickly found them all to be such a bore. The professors assigned everyone in class to do all of the same things everyday and as I would draw the contour of a piece of fruit on my sketchpad like the twelve other students sitting beside me, I began to wonder where my creativity was supposed to go.

***

Once in a painting class, our professor placed a tricycle, a gourd, and a skull sitting on the display. We were to focus on the shadows and the negative spaces. As we went about painting, I knew from the very beginning that I would not like what I was creating. The composition literally didn't make sense. What the heck was a gourd doing there next to a tricycle from the 1980's, not to mention a skull that looked as though it was straight out of a box of Halloween decorations? The assignment was so pointless to me. I was pessimistic and narrow. To do something without a reason or purpose was something I could not do. To simply work for a grade in itself was not enough of a reason for me. I knew well that my professor wanted me to learn the basic concepts of art, but I wanted to apply them to something bigger. Not a simple mash-up of things from a garage sale. I looked around and all of my classmates and sure enough, all of our paintings were quickly looking exactly the same. We were like robots creating cookie-cutter images, not art. A computer could have been programmed to do what I was doing sitting in that studio and my need to paint outside the lines was itching to break loose.

After most of the campus fell asleep that night, I walked back to the art building and threw away the work I had done during class. I took out a new sheet of canvas and began to paint away. I created a tricycle, but on the tricycle was a body of a gardener with the skull for its head. The figure had a gourd for a backpack and it was probably one of the most hilarious things I had ever seen. I sat back, laughed, and I knew I was satisfied. The painting made me smile, think, and wonder. I looked back on the requirements written on the overhead and I mentally checked them off the list,

- All three items must be present
- Careful precision of negative space
- Shows comprehension of the rules of shadows

As a week passed on by and I made my way back to class, I noticed the grade posted with scotch tape on top of my art, "C-".

"This was impressive, but it wasn't the assignment, Ji," my professor said as she was standing before me. She gave me a grim smile and it was insulting more than anything. Her posture was unenticing and her voice was desolate.

I walked straight out of the art studio that day and into the registrar's office to drop my art major and transferred into being a communications student. I wanted to communicate to people through art, not study art that didn't communicate at all.

***

Although I was satisfied with my drastic decision, I felt off. I was no longer pursuing what I had been so ambitious about and I began to wonder if anyone around me was actually content with the way their lives were going. I second-guessed every smile portrayed on my friends' faces and wondered the density of their laughter. College seemed so fake all of a sudden and that child-like vision I had of thinking creatively to better the world quickly began to fade.

It was then when positive people really began to drive me nuts. They were the people I loved to avoid. They weren't doing anything particularly wrong. It wasn't a personal attack on any specifically optimistic person. Truth be told, it was because I didn't believe any of them. Before becoming more aware of God, I wasn't sure about many things. But one thing I had no doubt about was that this world is messed up. And for someone to be ceaselessly happy in this uncompromisingly dim world seemed frightening and mad. It was either they were residing in a state of oblivion or they woke up lying to themselves everyday.

With this being said, I want to tell you about my friend, Bob. Like the many other influential people in my life, I also met Bob during my early years at Hope College. He is the reason why I will never look at a paintbrush the same again.

***

When I think of Bob, I think of raspberry ginger ale, golf hats, and pound cake. Welcome signs, scrambled eggs, and other fuzzy things of the like also come to mind. Bob lived in the assisted living facility for senior citizens in the downtown strip called The Warm Friend. He was also one of the brightest gentlemen on the block, literally. He wore pastels seven days per week. They were not the pastels that spoke: "Hello, I am richly involved in things like polo and croquet and I find myself at the Kentucky Derby just for kicks." They were more of the pastels that let you know: "I don't want to draw much attention to myself by wearing flashy colors, nor am I a fool to think that black is actually slimming. I've just had these shirts since the 80's and, to be frank, I don't sweat as much in yellow."

My friend, Grace (another Grace...yes, I had an oddly large amount of friends named Grace in my life), was a year below me as a stereotypically undecided freshman rummaging life to its core trying figure out her "calling" and Kylie was an avid nursing student bound to her near-perfect GPA. They were two of my greatest friends and they were just as anxious of college students as me. We'd drink tea to calm our nerves and we'd text each other cheesy quotes from *Winnie the Pooh* or *Friends* to ease another day of pressure from this world. But the only remedy that actually worked for us was Bob. Bob was another miracle placed in my life by the grace of God.

We would go visit the popular old man throughout each week and engage in various activities with him. There were months when painting was our "thing". Sometimes Bob would encourage us to write haikus about our feet or make a Christmas card in the month of June. Once, he told Kylie that he had always wanted to go up in a hot air balloon. So she took him. And he did. He went into the sky inside of a hot air balloon and waved from up on high to the ones who could see.

We met Bob because of a psychology class Grace was taking. She was assigned to visit a nursing home on a regular basis to take notes of the residents there and she happened to find herself making small conversation with Bob. That's just the kind of man Bob is; it's hard to pass by him without being captivated. She fell in love and told Kylie and me about who she had the privilege to visit. We quickly found ourselves taking turns stopping by the Warm Friend and giving Bob constant company. This was not because it was a charitable gesture on our part, but rather it being that all three of us always wanted to visit him...all the time. Taking turns was the only way he could have a little breather in between us crazy college kids.

His room was very small and on one of the highest floors of the building. The place itself was stuffy, but Bob's room—as enclosed as it was—seemed relatively breathable. On most days when I would go to surprise him, I'd find him sitting by his window, peering outside and observing the birds flying in the air. I'd ask if he wanted to turn on the television or care to watch a movie with me. He'd always decline and instead invite me to sit by the window and watch the birds with him. So I would. And each and every time, he made the better decision. He would share stories, drink his warm water, and pour the rest onto his plant he had growing by the windowsill. We'd breathe in the scents of the seasons and make up names for the people walking below us because we could. I enjoyed so many things about Bob's nature and the ways in which he'd calm my soul. He allowed me to release the stresses I had from school, parents, friends, society, and life by not probing me at all. He just allowed me to be.

***

In the beginning of one week, Bob was working on a series of bird paintings. What I found most peculiar about them was that they always had a background. It was never just the bird. The bird would be flying away from a scenery of buildings or forests. The bird was always active; always so detached. Toward the end of the same week, he worked on the extended the series with butterflies. They were flying away, too. His winged creations were always flying away. Always smiling. Always so, so colorful and carefree. The colors were out of this world and his painting didn't always make sense. I then shared with him my fears of creating outside the expectations of the world and he told me I was being silly. He told me the world would always tell me different. He told me not to care. It was as simple as that.

"Teachers don't know everything," Bob said, "Trust me; I used to be one. They just jumped through all of the right hoops. Don't get me wrong; there are plenty great ones out there. But even with people in authority…here's what you do. Respect them; obey them…but no one's forcing you to agree with them. Until your day comes, just keep moving on and don't forget to keep your chin up."

I looked at my rebellious friend with a surprised face and asked, "Bob, where did you teach?"

He smirked at me and responded with grace, "Where you are struggling now. At Hope College."

I painted my sky in shades of red and purple that day.

***

What I loved most about Bob was his undeniable conviction in God. I don't remember when exactly I found out he was a believer. Now that I think about it, I don't think he ever actually told me. It was vivid and obvious from the way he would love others...from the way he would love me. He loved in such a way that there was no question that it was the love of Jesus pouring out from his transparent heart. He never complained. He never cared to. It was a love and a joy so out of this world. Bob lived his life as a free man. Like the way his birds and his butterflies in his paintings would be so distant from the cityscapes below, Bob's soul lingered above what most of us were so caught up in. He flew with wings stretched out and he let the things below be.

***

Another time I visited with Grace, Bob showed us a book he had written. He constantly surprised us with new things; no one knew he wrote. The title of the book was *Happy Bob*. Inside, he only wrote moments in his life that he found himself happy and pictures to capture what he felt. That was it. It was never sold. He said he wrote it because he needed to remember the good things in his life. It was more for himself than anything. It was colorful, out of order, and in very large print. It was the best picture book I'd ever read.

I told him that day that I also wished to write a book one day, I just didn't know about what. I asked Bob if he had any helpful hints or advice, and this is what Bob said to me,

"If you ever do write a book, Ji—which you will—just make sure you make the cover whatever you want, not what anyone else tells you. No matter what we want to say, we all know that people judge books by their cover. You might as well make it represent your story well. Paint it the way you see the world. Like you've always wanted to."

I laughed, "Okay. But Bob, what if I want to put a piece of fruit on it?"

"Then put a piece of fruit on it. And make it a weird one."

***

A few months ago, Bob breathed his last breath here with us at the glorious age of ninety-one. I didn't cry that day because I knew he went with peace in his heart. He didn't waste a single moment dwelling in the sorrows of death; he lived every moment relishing the joys of life.

Bob had joy in the depths of his heart because he learned long ago that what others thought of his soul did not matter with God. And after the first few minutes of knowing Bob, it was obvious that God was the only one he was concerned about pleasing. And in order to please God, we simply need to enjoy the life He has given us in the way He had always meant for us to enjoy it..

I guess there aren't simply "happy people" and "sad people". Positive or not, there are just people. We're all just people and we live through conditions and seasons. We get a chance to decide what we are everyday. We also have a chance to renew. I decided on the day Bob said goodbye to the world that I will choose joy as often as I could. Anyone can be grumpy. It's easy to stay bitter. It takes courage to be something as creative and out of this world to be optimistic. In all seasons, we have the option to fall down with the rain or sing praise about the fact that we can taste it. And I will choose to taste the rain. I will choose to live my life. I will choose to paint my skies the brightest colors I can find that day because life is but a moment and to live with a freed spirit is to live forever. Thank you, Bob. Rest in peace.

Chapter Ten:
Define Success

Sixth grade was when I had first declared a "favorite" book. It was about a thirteen-year-old boy with divorced parents who, on his way to visit his father in Canada, gets into an airplane crash and finds himself stranded and alone with nothing for survival other than the gift he had received from his mother before the trip. It was his hatchet. A small and powerful tool kept in his back pocket. The book was, believe it or not, titled, *Hatchet,* by Gary Paulsen. I enjoyed this book because it introduced to me a new place in my mind that I didn't know existed. It made me wonder about basic survival, something that absolutely fascinated me.

If you ask me now, I think about survival quite often, especially in this day and age. It is not that I spend time thinking about it in a way where it is a worry. I think about it because it amazes me how constantly refined it is by a new ultimatum set by standards of man, not innate survival in itself. It seems to be that even as affluent as the first-world nations have come to be, we have stayed unimpressively stagnant in the confidence of persevering. If we are to take any child privileged enough to be enrolled in an education system today and inform him or her that there was no way for them to find a job by the end of jumping through these hoops, he or she would be devastated. They would ponder their ability to survive. They wouldn't know how to use a hatchet even if it were in their back pockets and to be frank, I think many would rather choose to fail at surviving than to know their ego and pride would be stripped. This form and idea of survival is much different than the boy in *The Hatchet*'s. We really are dramatic around here.

***

For the longest time, my definition of success truly did struggle between aligning itself with being able to find three meals per day to being able to juggle a fancy façade I learned to wear so well on campus. I was a poor girl amongst the circumstances of the rich and no one knew it except for me and God Himself. With my heart on my sleeve, I was attending one of the most expensive colleges in the Midwest while my wealthy classmates and professors had no idea that I had not paid a single penny to the institution yet.

While digging a deep and endless hole of student debt, I constantly found myself whispering to my conscience it was going to be worth it at the end. I would think about giving my parents an all-expense paid vacation after I made it big so they could rest for the first time in their hardworking lives. I relished ideas like going to third-world countries and personally feeding a child so that I could know what it's like to make a difference. I dwelled in dreams where I didn't have to wonder where I was going to get my next bite of food. I dwelled in dreams where my concern was no longer monetary issues, but the issues of the heart.

Then came my last semester of college. I was told out of the blue by the financial aid services that I was not going to be able to come back to finish my degree and graduate due to issues dealing with money. Also during the same month, I had landed a post-college job with Young Life, a nationwide non-profit organization I had come to love while volunteering with them since I first moved over to Holland. I was going to serve with them on the West Coast after walking across that graduation stage. It was one of the most bizarre moments of my life and it was absolutely out of my control.

When studying at Hope College, one of the greatest lessons I had learned was that there is no such thing as a bad circumstance if God is in the picture. Throughout that following week, I had a lot of time to think.

I spent the nights awake and prayed often in these silent moments. I thought back to who I was when I entered college and the person who I had become. In my time of reflection, I laughed. I laughed a lot. The amount of change I underwent was drastic, ridiculous, and possible only by God Himself. I remembered how tense I used to be. And here I was with an overwhelming sense of peace at the fact that I might not even finish what I had invested three and a half years of my life in.

The truth is, I have come to find that when we feel the most stuck in life is when we should move away from that place in our hearts. There are times when we ought to be fervent in our prayers. Then there are times when we should realize perhaps we ought to change the how we are praying all together. Some might disagree to say that one ought to stick it out and fight back. But when all doors slam shut and stay locked for an extensive amount of time, we shouldn't be so oblivious to think that God isn't sending us a sign that He might just have something better in mind. Like many things that need art and balance, this is definitely one of them. I knew I wasn't the only one praying that I would come out of college successfully and willfully. My mother had been praying for it since she first knew how and I was very much aware at this point that God never neglects to listen to us. He hears it all but He also knows far past our horizons. And when He tells us things that He knows better, we shouldn't stand in His way out of spite and fear. It may not have made sense, but I knew I was going to be okay because God was allowing it to happen. It wasn't a lack of perseverance and it most certainly wasn't giving up; it was surrendering to what will be. It was letting go of pride.

Before making things final and leaving for home that Christmas break—the break that changed my life forever—I was heavily advised to go meet a mentor. Several different friends directed me to the same person and I actually ended up knowing the guy. I had been introduced to the man in my early years of college. He was pretty much an adult rock star on campus. He was a father to many and a friend to all. He wore flowers on his shirts and joy was his favorite perfume. People would go to him for advice extending from silly breakups to spiritual warfare. I hoped this topic was no more or less in his range.

I set up a meeting not too long after I had become aware of my circumstance and as I began to explain my situation, he listened patiently with a genuine concern. I knew he cared and I knew he meant well, but by the end of our conversation, he was thoroughly displeased with where I stood about it all.

"Ji. I appreciate your optimistic perspective on life. It really is refreshing and most certainly rare. But I can't help but needing to ask, aren't you the least bit concerned about how you're going to make it out there?" He stood up from his leather chair and began to walk in the pattern-8 as he tapped the end of his pen on his forehead, "I mean, a college degree is basically one's only way for survival these days. Dropping out with just a few credits left is a detrimental idea. I get it that there doesn't seem to be a way for you right now, but gosh... I mean, there's just gotta be, you know? We gotta keep searching. And maybe just...I'm so sorry about this. Maybe we can—"

"No. I'm not," I interjected, "And I'm not sorry."

He stopped pacing and looked down at me, "I'm sorry, dear?"

"That's just it, sir. I'm not sorry about it," I said again, "I don't know. Maybe it is a foolish choice. But it's not really a choice either. It's what is up ahead for me in my life and if that is the way things are meant to be, I can't help but think that grieving and denying the truth is much more detrimental to both my health and survival. I am so thankful for your wisdom and your concern but in all honesty I mean it when I say I am not worried. I'm going to be just fine. It's going to be okay. I will survive. I know what to dig out of my back pocket."

With a kind hug and a meaningful smile, he escorted me out of his office and I waved my potential alma mater goodbye. I thought about the last thing I said to him and I must admit, I thought it was pretty cool. I thought it was cool that even a story I read in sixth grade affected my decision-making to this day and that it was radical that life is but an assortment of endless poetry. I found my very own hatchet in depths of my college years and it was Jesus. To survive was to know that even in temporary trials such as this, I had a heart that would persevere and a body that would move forward. I didn't know the guarantees of tomorrow but I didn't need them. I had what I needed for today and that was all I could ask for. I didn't come to college to learn about art or communications; I came to college to learn about life. And I did, I learned about Life.

I had a job in the bag that I was absolutely passionate about, the best friends I could ever ask for, and hope for the future because I could picture Jesus there with me, wherever it was. My identity was no longer in the sights of others. My identity and self-worth was in the sight of God and I knew I was capable. If this circumstance taught me one thing, it was that I have finally realized that my identify finally was not attached to my worldly successes. This was one of the most liberating realizations in the world. I was capable to walk away from this conversation with an abundance of grace and peace and that was something I had not learned before attending Hope College. And what I have realized is that I wasn't at this school to learn about a specific study, I was there to learn about life. All of the other stuff, to me, was not learning how to survive. That was for dead fish in the stream going with the flow with the many other dead fish who have lived before them.

I came to college to learn. I came to explore my potential and to broaden my perspective. I came to meet people of all sorts and to gather ways to engage with the rest of this world. I desired to become equipped socially, emotionally, and spiritually, and at that point, I honestly felt more ready than ever. A piece of document worth thousands of dollars telling me whether I am worth it or not meant nothing to me. I felt very much equipped to go become more of who I was meant to be in the world waiting outside my door. When it came down to it all, I got what I needed. I got what I came for. I didn't need a college degree to tell me I was competent and I honestly didn't know why I allowed the world to tell me otherwise for so long.

***

My friend Dave threw a bonfire that night.

We talked about the potentials that the upcoming summer held and where all of our friendships would go. We ate a few s'mores, dropped most of them into the fire actually, and we spoke out loud our dreams while shuddering with excitement and fear at the same time. With hours passing, conversation branched farther and farther out. I looked around at my friends and asked, "Who do you think you would have been the closest of friends with in the Bible?"

There was a moment for thought and resonation.

Our intellect, Noah, finally spoke, "Like, who do we think we would have spent these kinds of bonfires with?"

I imagined all of us as bearded men in gladiator-style sandals sitting around the fire with even more men with beards and gladiator-style sandals as we ate fish and probably dropped most of the into the fire.

I looked over at him and chuckled, "More or less, Noah. I'm wondering who you guys think you would've related with the most."

A bit more of silence entered the atmosphere.

"Thomas," Dave suddenly said, "Doubting Thomas."

This came across as a shock, I think, for most of us. Dave, at least to me, has always come off as such a dignified and confident person of faith. I never questioned his standing on God, let alone take the time to wonder or ask if he had struggles with doubt. In the Bible, Thomas is quite a fascinating character, one most can relate with because he calls Jesus out and is then humbled when He allows Thomas to touch the holes in His hands from where He once was nailed and hung on the cross for us.

"I think, if anything, I'd secretly want to hang out with Thomas because I'm secretly jealous of him. I know that sounds wrong, but it's true. I'm so jealous that he got to experience something so crazy like that. I mean, can you even imagine?"

I really couldn't imagine. That was nuts.

Our friend Erin said she would want to chill with Peter. She said she would want to be influenced by people so daring enough to walk out onto water like he did when Jesus invited him to do so.

"I don't know what it's like to have that kind of faith," Erin said, "I definitely think I could learn a thing or two from the guy."

"And, well, what about you?" Dave asked, "I'm sure you didn't ask that question without having someone in mind yourself."

These friends of mine knew me too well.

"I wish I could be best friends with Paul," I said, "He seems to get it, you know?"

I looked around the fire and everyone waited.

"I mean, even in the times when he is imprisoned and stuck, he didn't allow his soul to be imprisoned nor stuck. In my personal opinion, he is the freest man in the Bible next to Jesus. He needed nothing because he had everything. And everything he needed was something no one could take away. I feel like that is truly something worth aiming for. He knew what his ultimate goal in life was and, I think, he had already succeeded. By the end of it all, he was glad that he could even be in prison, or not, or where ever God placed him to be. He understood what it meant to find joy in life. He lived his life for others to be able to grasp that kind of joy. He knew all else would be just fine. What was out of his hands was out of his hands. While people were feeling sorry for him, he was feeling sorry for others 'cuz they simply couldn't get it. This is the kind of joy I want to live for, too. The kind that goes against all currents of this world."

***

Three days after, something amazing happened. I received an e-mail from The New York Times asking if I wanted to take up a position as a travel photographer. A few moments after gawking at the e-mail, I then received a phone call from a firm in Indianapolis asking if I was interested in a graphic design position. I questioned how they had heard about me and they happily replied that a trustworthy client referred them my name and contact information. And by the time I checked my e-mail again within the same hour, there was an inquiry by a corporate company from the Holland area seeking out my resume for a potential candidate as director of communications, also implying that they would pay off the rest of any education I needed to finish.

I had not sent in one job application to these places.

It didn't make sense. I know. But I still have the e-mails saved. And that phone call is still remembered by my friends who were nearby. It all happened and I don't really know why.

Or maybe I do know why.

***

I met up with a friend that day at the City Delicatessen and I told him the latest news while I chomped on my Denver sandwich. After we laughed, made a scene, and looked at one another, he shook his head with disbelief.

"So you're going to take up one of those offers, right?"

"Nah. I already found a job I love, remember?"

"Ji, as a friend who cares about you and your future, can I say that's a real stupid idea? Take one of these jobs that'll actually get you a paycheck!"

"None taken," I said with a smile, "And no. I'd rather be poor in paper money and rich in passion rather than abundant in artificial comfort and dead in my faith any day."

He raised his brow a bit and pointed his fork at me, "Alright, but let me ask you something. How in the *world* do these opportunities land so stinkin' effortlessly on your lap from all sorts of directions? No offense. But I legitimately do not understand your luck!"

I simply smirked behind my long, messy hair and replied, "Because it's out of this world. And it's not luck; it's God."

* Spoiler alert: the rest of the *Hatchet* story goes so that the main character ends up finding some excess resources that had crashed with the plane. There was extra food and a rifle. It also included a transmitter that allows him to eventually go home. But he didn't need any of this stuff anymore; he could survive. He could survive well. He had his will, his heart, and his well-used hatchet he kept in his back pocket.

Chapter Eleven:
I'm Sorry

I met one of my closest friends in a philosophy class a few years back. Lydia and I both would both snooze off to the same ancient theories and wake up to the sound of the same ruler being angrily hit on the head table. To this day I am sure that our professor still tells horror stories about us two sleepyheads in his lecture halls. It's rather funny how God chooses to place people in our lives. She is now someone who I hold very near to my heart and is a friend who gives me proof on a daily basis that we were never meant to live this life alone. Aside from teaching me about Indiana University's basketball history and constantly informing me on how to eat gluten-free at restaurants when we're not actually gluten-free, Lydia has also taught me throughout the years that in order to find mutual ground with others, vulnerability must exist within the relationship. I think this is why it took me so long to know that I was not the only one with the struggles I had in this world. I had a hard time opening up to the people around me. Lydia did not hesitate to always take the first step of this in our friendship. I guess I never realized how rare this was until she came into my life. She was different. She was true.

***

Once, I had the strangest conversation with her. It was by far one of the strangest conversations of my life and by far one of the best. It was strange because it was unpredictable, unfamiliar, and uncommon. It was the best because it taught me one of the most important lessons there is to learn.

We were hanging out together on a Sunday night and it was about a month shy from Christmas. I was well on my way of entering the last holiday break of my college career and the last thing anyone was doing on campus was studying. Lydia and I attended our regular Gathering service—an evening event held during the school year at Hope College—and we lingered within the pews of the beautiful Dimnent Chapel in our sweatpants because we had homework to do. It may have been an insensible idea but lingering was more of appealing than finding the p-value of any statistical data that night.

***

Lydia and I sat at the very top of the balcony and breathed in the quietness of the architecture until the janitorial staff compliantly shut off the lights. It was not in our intentions to stay past hours but since we were already found ourselves there, we stayed even longer.

Everything was still.

But not everything was settled.

I believe there to be two kinds of silences. There is the kind of silence where its roots resonate peace and tranquility. It is very purposeful and it would almost be rude to break it. I remember my friend Jared once told me that to engage in this type of silence with a friend is to taste the bread and butter of a solid friendship. It is supposedly a marvelous and unique experience to have with others because it most often speaks louder about the freedom and contentment in your relationship than any eloquent words could tell. Then, there is the kind of silence that is filled with anticipatory notes. It is the silence that keeps us from making the next move or feeling confident in the pace in which things are moving. It is also the reason we always invite that overly talkative friend of ours to new and awkward outings because we can only take so much of this anxiety-filled silence with others until being present in that moment was not worth it at all.

Lydia and I hardly ever faced the latter type of silence while together. But in this moment, I was certain we were immersed in it. I could sense it from the second it had entered. While we sat and waited timidly in the empty building, I felt as though I was literally hitting the silent anticipatory notes with a gong.

"Okay, I need to ask you something," Lydia finally blurted.

"Yeah, certainly."

I let go of my breath and thanked God it wasn't me.

I could hear Lydia taking her jacket off and readjusting the way she was sitting. As her breathing settled down, the noise in the air alleviated itself.

"I want to ask you for your forgiveness," Lydia whispered.

It took me a moment to understand what she had said. And even after that moment, I still wasn't quite sure of it. There was absolutely nothing I could think of in our history where this gesture seemed necessary.

"Lyds, you didn't—"

"No. Listen."

So I did. I listened as patiently as I could.

She began to explain to me all the things she had done in the past that might not have resembled the notion of a good friend. She then confessed to me the times in which negative thoughts regarding anything I had ever done or said had flooded into her mind but she had never revealed. She started apologizing for the moments she had left me wounded but she could have been completely unaware of. And lastly, she asked if I would forgive her for the times she would wrong me in the future.

I didn't know how many people did this, asking for forgiveness regarding deeds no one knew about, let alone ones that have not been committed yet. Most people would've found this absurd and completely irrational. But then again, I had never heard a more sincere apology in my life. It came straight from her heart with no filters, constraints, or hesitation.

It was not confusion I felt, nor was it anything uncertain. It was in this moment where God spoke clear to me that I was sitting next to someone who knew Him well. No one had ever apologized to me for their poor thoughts or transgressions in their hearts.

It may have sounded crazy, but I understood her. It was easy to hear what she had to say because she had absolutely no walls for me to read or work through. Everything about her was transparent and completely vulnerable. She admittedly confessed through her apology that she was, indeed, human. I didn't know if this was something I could willingly confess to others. I never really gave much thought about it. To be flawed and imperfect was the last thing I'd want to talk about. I never would have sought to accept that it was in my nature. And yet here she was, testifying the blunt and honest truth that she is capable of messing up and letting me know that she was well aware of it.

While being in absolute captivity of her ability to find her identity in God and not in my opinion of her or her past actions, my all due respect for Lydia skyrocketed to an immeasurable degree. How was it that someone professing their weaknesses made them appear that much more courageous and more confident? She redefined for me what it meant to be brave. For all of my life, I thought I'd been strong by not letting anyone in. Transparency was a concept I paralleled with the weak and I built walls around my heart to stay away from this very idea. But in that moment, I was made confident that I was wrong. I was figuring out that to be vulnerable and exposed is the noblest thing of all.

"Yes," I stammered, "yes, of course I forgive you."

"No, I need you to look at me," I had never heard Lydia speak so sternly, "I need you to see that I mean it."

I looked toward my earnest friend and I could make her face out even amongst the darkness. I could see the sincerity through her big brown eyes.

"I forgive you," I told her.

With the small light that was scandalously peaking in from the moon hung outside, I could witness the joy overflowing from her as she gave me the biggest smile of affirmation.

***

I laid in bed that night going over our weird conversation. I kept wondering if it was necessary. I had no doubt in my mind that it was good. But I wasn't sure if I deserved it; I wasn't sure what triggered such an act.

It may sound crazy, but it made me think about my biological father. As my eyes adjusted to the dark and stared at the patterns on my ceiling, I began to feel queasy and perplexed. This was the first time I thought about my biological father since he disappeared from my life when I was four. He never crossed my mind prior to this spontaneous conversation with Lydia. That might also sound completely insane but it is true. I would sometimes even forget that my stepfather wasn't my real dad. It wasn't because he was any more warm or inviting. It was simply because he was physically existent in my life while I had not even a trace of what my biological father's face looked like.

The whole concept of a father figure was a mystery to me. I literally knew nothing about mine except for the fact that I still carried around his last name. I could only remember his black socks because they were all I could see during the night he struck my mother and walked away for good.

I thought about my father because if there was anybody out there who I would have felt the need to have a conversation with like the one I just had with Lydia, it would have been with him. In such unexplainable ways, I felt like he needed to know that I forgave him. I wished so badly that night regardless of where ever he was in this world, that I could look him in the eyes and make sure he understood that he was set free. That he didn't need to be held captive by the past or the future. That he was a forgiven man.

In an even more unexplainable way, I wished to tell him that I was sorry. Not because it was necessary or because he deserved it, but simply because I was. I was sorry about the man he might have wanted to be and the one this world kept him from being. I was sorry about what pains he might have gone through while never knowing his own daughter and what lies he must have told himself in order to endure. And I was sorry that he was such an insignificant part of my childhood that I had come to a point where he had essentially been erased from existence. What a sad thing to be a nobody in someone's world. The man I shared DNA with was obsolete in my life and it never occurred to me that it could be killing somebody.

And maybe he didn't care at all. Maybe his life has been but a dream since the day we went separate ways. But that didn't seem to matter to me all of a sudden. It wasn't in the fact that he expected an apology or a need for such a conversation. It was in the fact that it was important to me and I allowed the truth to set me free.

***

Something tells me that Lydia would have been just fine even if I did not forgive her that night. In retrospect, I believe she did it for herself as much as she did it for me. It was releasing, redeeming, and gaining much deserved dignity. I think she did it because she knew she was sitting right with God and to execute her apology toward me was but the punctuation to a breath of inescapably fresh air. Her satisfaction did not rely on what my reaction was, but rather that she said what she needed to say and I was open to hearing it. She took an opportunity and used it. The rest was out of her control and that was completely okay. Her satisfaction was already made full in God; my friendship was but an extra blessing.

For most of my life, the concepts of grace and forgiveness were exempt. I grew up being taught that in order to win, one must stay on top. And in order to stay on top, one must never give in. Grace was a virtue that went right over my head and forgiveness was an idea I never desired to fancy. I think it's because with these virtues, love is both the exception and the rule. I think I never understood any of it fully because I never understood love.

Lydia taught me one of the most important lessons of my life that night. I never knew the power of grace and forgiveness until I found myself undergoing it so directly and reluctantly. I didn't realize this could be so much of the reason why I had felt so much weight on my shoulders in my yesteryears. I never knew what it was like to truly forgive others in my life. To truly love them was to truly forgive them and to truly forgive is to forget what was once before. I never really knew how to do this. I never knew how to love ceaselessly. This revelation during my last few days at Hope College quickly led up to what happened last Christmas, a night that changed my life forever.

***

Last Christmas, we were very much into the depths of Michigan winter and my post-college plans did not begin until the end of spring. My preparation was all off and it came to a point where I had nowhere to move into for the time being other than back home in Grand Rapids with my mother and stepfather. This was more or less of an awkward situation seeing as how I hardly made a point to visit within my years of being at school. It became a rude habit of mine to become detached with what was once familiar and before I knew it, it was uncomfortable to ask if I could come back after years of what appeared to be abandonment.

When I left for college after graduating high school, there were ugly words thrown from both ends along with an agreement to not agree ever. About anything. About career paths. About college degrees. About boyfriends and any life choices that would matter. I went to an institution they were not gung-ho about and they told me they expected me to at least become a doctor when I came back. I responded that I never asked for such wonderful support in the first place and that I would become a starving artist on the streets just to rub some extra dirt in it. In spite of one another, we lived ridiculous family dynamics and everything about moving back in made me want to throw up my nerves.

I was a changed woman, a proud child of God, and I honestly had no idea where I had left things with my family. I also had no idea why I thought it was okay never to resolve. Maybe I assumed this day would never have to come. So much of who I was and what I believed changed since leaving for Hope College and I didn't know what it looked like to interact in old settings with a new soul. A part of me wanted to act as though nothing had changed for the sake of easy transition. They expected the same Ji they once knew and it would take a miracle to convince them I was different. Yet this idea of resuming to the ugly past tortured me, too. I didn't want to be that daughter my parents once knew. Everything about it seemed so immature and unimportant now. I wanted to reintroduce myself again and I wanted to tell them so badly that I want to started over. I wished to shake hands with them and tell them, "I'm Ji, and you know nothing about who I am." But that's the kind of stuff you do with acquaintances, not lifelong family members. Lifelong family members will always know you for who you have been, not who you have become.

Still, I didn't want to run away anymore. I was moving in that Christmas break and I was done forsaking people because of the things the devil would whisper in my ear. I wanted to end this vicious cycle of generational patterns of abandonment and shame spewing into all sorts of unnecessary directions. To my surprise, as well as the ones around me, I decided to say something so weird that Christmas night. Weird enough to change everything.

***

It has never been in our family tradition to celebrate anything in a super big way. Even with Christmas, the showiest thing we'd ever done was getting caramelized walnuts for our holiday salad one year. Once we started attending church, it became commonplace to start off Christmas Eve with the congregation. But our family would usually keep things low key on Christmas day itself with no extended family to welcome due to the fact that they all lived in South Korea. My parents often found themselves moseying back into work by the time noon rolled around to get extra cleaning done. Then Jasmin and I would be left just the two of us which usually led to us in crawling back into our pajamas and turning on our yearly showing of the fuzzy VHS versions of Home Alone I and II as we'd fall asleep before anyone could say, "Merry Christmas, ya filthy animal!"

On this Christmas night, however, we were all home for dinner. This was a pretty amazing circumstance. We were about to eat when my mother stood up at the head of the table, "We should say grace together...should we not? I mean, it is Jesus' birthday, for goodness' sake."

I was as shocked, humbled, and absolutely impressed.

"I can't," I then blurted. I told you I said something weird. What did you say?"

"I can't, until I say something first."

My mother and stepfather sat there and stared while Jasmin stood awkwardly with silverware in her hands, debating whether or not to place them at the table and almost doing a form of dance with her longing to finish her task and to be socially appropriate at the same time.

"If I'm going to move back in, there are few things I must say," I looked toward my parents as they kept their arms crossed and bodies stiff, "I know it hasn't been fair...the way I left things. But in this time, I've learned a lot. And I think the biggest thing I have realized is that...I don't know much at all."

And this is when I told them everything. I told them about my past and the memories I had kept hidden from their awareness. I reminded them of the words that had been spoken, hearts that have been broken, and the times I lacked the courage and the maturity to know otherwise. I told them about when I was suicidal, when death was a constant whisper in my ear and how I grappled with an eating disorder while I was very much under their roof because I wanted to make them proud. I also then revealed revelations I have experienced and life-changing events that had occurred in my life since I had moved out from home. I told them about faith and my search of hope that had altered all things. I talked about how my passions and desires in life have changed and what kind of person I now aim to be. And most importantly, I told them about my new relationship with God. I told them about change and grace. I told them every depth of my heart and it poured out like a waterfall after an icy, long winter.

I looked down at my shaking hands and I looked back up at my family, "I can't live under a roof where there is no room for people to see me for who I am. I am no longer who I used to be. I can't give thanks to our Savior on His birthday unless it's with an upright heart and I can't seem to consider myself deemed as such unless I ask for your forgiveness. So here I am. I'm sorry. With all of my heart, I am sorry. For all that I have done, for all the pain I might have caused, for the past mistakes and for the ones in the future. I am sorry because I had forgotten somewhere along the way that we are family and that was wrong of me. I am sorry for forgetting. I am sorry for not knowing then. I ask for your forgiveness. I hope you can hear my heart."

I had tears in my eyes and they felt hot as they made a stream down my face.

Then my mother spoke, "You are forgiven."

I looked at her and she was crying. I began to wonder what she had been going through. A great gust of curiosity rushed inside me as I pondered on what she had been dealing with, the things unspoken...the things a daughter never knows.

Then she spoke once more, "You're forgiven, as long as you can forgive me, too."

That's when I knew. I had never loved my family right because I had never forgiven them in my heart. This entire time—even as we began to attend church and make changes—these behaviors were but bandages continuing to build upon a thick layer of lies because the core had not been healed. And in this moment, I felt a release. As I spoke the words, "I forgive you," to my mother, it was as though my soul had broken out of chains and for the first time in my life, I could see my parents as how God sees them; pure, beloved, and absolutely precious. I couldn't tell you the last time I had sincerely given them a hug. As I approached my mother, my I noticed my stepfather's face grew weary.

"You must forgive me, too," he said.

"I forgive you, too," I replied.

And I meant it. Nothing else needed to be spoken. Nothing else needed to be done. The memories that used to haunt me everyday escaped through the vanished barriers of my mind and all the things that were so sore and bitter...the things in my life that I honestly thought I could never recover from...they were healed. Somehow by the grace of His timing, this Christmas break when I moved back home altered everything about our family in ways that countered all that I'd once known.

***

We need to give each other grace because we just don't know when and how God changes people. People will never be able to change in our lives if we don't allow them to in our hearts. And the reality is, they usually do change with time. We just have to see it. They never stay the same person because we all go through trials that produce growth. I hope that we don't wish idleness in anyone. I hope we anticipate growth and change in those of us we interact with. It is not so much as to whether or not we love them as the person we met when we first did, but whether or not we love the God who has created them and constantly refines their hearts. Because that is the only consistent thing we will find in this world; the Jesus working within each and every one of us. And at this point with my family, we were all hanging onto the same rope and that rope of hope was God. We were one. It took twenty-one years, but for the first time in my life, I found myself in love with my family. And this time, I know I always will.

We made a promise that night. We promised one another we would pray together as often as we could. Although uncomfortable and many times inconvenient, we made a point since that day to meet on a weekly basis, at least, whether via phone or in person, to share our burdens and to keep one another in the loop of how we are in relation to God who brought us together.

***

In the end, we really are just a bunch of people who try are trying our best, we really are. Indeed we mess up as much as the next person, but that's why we are not a bunch of people worshipping ourselves. Because I am sure that I will mess up again. I will let the people around me down, and sometimes, I won't even know it.

With that being said, I want to say that I'm sorry to you, the reader. Wherever you find yourself right now as you are holding this book, I hope you know I am thinking about you as I write this. I'm sorry for all the times you were supposed to hear this but you weren't told. On behalf of every person who has messed up without knowing it and will indeed mess it up again, I'm sorry. Because you deserve to hear it, and you deserve to know that someone cares. I think you deserve to know that you are forgiven, too. You are forgiven by the One who loved you first. You are forgiven, as long as you can accept that kind of grace. I also pray that you are able to extend this kind of grace to others. Watch it rock your world. Watch it bring your family together. Watch it save your life.

Chapter Twelve:
People Are People

A while ago, there was a video that went viral in the social media realm. I was online and a link posted by a friend grabbed my attention because of its attractive thumbnail. You'd think I'd have a mental filter for that by now. But nope, I clicked it. To be honest, I had no idea what the link was about. I was putting off some photography work and finding random YouTube clips was more than ideal. But the moment I pressed 'play', I felt a form of regret. It was a pretty lengthy segment of this North Korean refugee who was talking in front of a mass audience. She was pale, kind, and soft-spoken. She was also very skinny. It was not the kind of skinny one aims for when he or she is obsessively on a treadmill and eating half of a leaf per day. It was the kind of skinny that didn't choose to be there. It was the kind that expressed outwardly one's inward trials and heartaches.

Usually when I would see documents and articles about North Korea, I seldom leaned in. I knew it was something I could have personally worked on as a civil human being, but I thought of it as an insolvable issue. I had grown up with its history haunting me all of my life and I eventually came to a point where I saw that it did very little for me to voice my personal opinions on.

***

When I lived in South Korea, the main talk of the streets outside the local bakeries and newsstands would be the never-ending bickering of young adults getting so caught up and frustrated about how much they couldn't stand North Korea. I would hear shouts and uproars on a daily basis about how unfortunate it is that our thriving country had to share the same chunk of geographical land with them.

I knew it was a big deal. And I knew there were some people making poor decisions out there. But as much as I felt thankful to live in a free country like ours, I had an even stronger feeling that speaking unkind words and frowning a lot wouldn't solve much. To me, the folks talking about this concern looked more or less like bigots. They talked about others as though they were trash. I hated that. Sure, people can be annoying sometimes. And I understood that what was happening with North Korea was far more than just "annoying". But by the end of the day, people were people. People weren't things, especially not trash. I remember pretending to be too young to understand. I'd smile nonchalantly as I'd scat away from these arguments and as fast as I could.

Even moving to the United States, the issue was still lingering in my backyard. I wasn't aware at the time how grand of a problem it was. I guess bombs really freaked people out, no matter where you lived. And even then, it still seemed like nonsense to me. It all seemed like chaos and nonsense. If I knew my life was on the line from a bomb threat or even some disease or old age, I hoped I wouldn't find myself wasting my time hating others and having complaints dribble out of my mouth, but rather loving others with words to express the things I hope to stand by when I'm gone.

But no. All I could hear was hate. Hate, bickering, hate. I heard the same bickering and unkind words, just in a different language. The frowns were just as ugly. It never left. Hate was everywhere, including in the words of my new classmates. If I could have been handed a dollar for every time I was asked if I was North or South Korean, I would have none because I would have spent that huge amount of money buying a Culture and Ethics 101 book for all who would need to ask. The amount of ignorance in foreign policies of my American peers slayed me in the worst ways. And yet I couldn't blame them either. It was as though the concept of North Korea was sucking away the joy in all of what surrounded me in the most miniscule but obnoxious ways while growing up. When the topic would arise, I'd be the first to exit the room. I didn't care. I didn't want it to bother me. I just wanted people to know that I was Ji and although there is a country with malnourished people and a heavily confused dictator, I personally preferred engaging in healthy conversations with kinder people about things that can actually change the world, not the things we didn't seem to be doing much to resolve.

As I still found myself with this video clip playing before my eyes, I could not help but notice the amount of hits it had thus far. It reached well over one million views and it had been available for less than a day. As much as I didn't want to engage, I found this to be rather strange. I was curious why people were so absorbed. I continued watching as I slowly let go of the idea of that I'd actually get work done.

The young woman was explaining how she had escaped her country and what her walk has been like through the indescribable years of running away and hiding. The brokenness of her English automatically tuned my heart with hers because this is how I often heard my parents. I felt like I was listening to my parents in a weird way. Whether one was speaking with a South or North Korean accent, it was still not the fluid English language, the one my brain could take in the easiest. I always had to readjust the settings in my head to understand my parents clearly when communicating with them and I found myself doing the same for her. This woman was trying so hard to accommodate and bring clarity to the messages that she so desperately desired to share. And yet this barrier of linguistics stood so tall and broad amongst us all. It kept us from truly hearing the heart.

In the middle of her speech, I observed a slight change in her eyes. It was as though her remarks were no longer coming from a rehearsed and thoroughly thought through exhibition, but rather it was coming from somewhere within soul and not her busy mind. She began to speak about how she came to a place in her life where she no longer knew herself. She explained that she did not know which country she felt loyal to because she had run away from everything she had known and yet called so many of them "home" for a temporary time. She did not know whom to call as family or what to really call herself. If I didn't know any better, this was no longer a presentation on the issues of North Korea or immigration policies; this was a heart crying out from a darker corner of loneliness and confusion.

And in that moment, I knew her heart was heard. I began to understand why this video seemed to collect so many views and positive feedback. It spoke to people. It wasn't a political schema or a debate. It was a real person talking about their real trials of the heart. It surpassed the social boundaries of looks, language, history, or circumstance. Her message was heard by the cloud of witnesses amongst her and this was because what she described was not that uncommon of a life story. It was a story of every soul that has lived through being human. This loss of identity. A wonder of self-worth. The confusion of purpose and truth.

I wanted so badly to reach across my computer screen and give this woman a hug. I wanted to tell her that she was not alone and that none of what she had to go through was her fault. But all I could do was just sit there and stare. I prayed to God she was in a better place now. I prayed to God she found her home.

***

Christians often speak of this concept of being *in* this world but not *of* this world. They also speak about how our citizenship is in heaven and not here on earth. This kind of talk always seemed like bologna to me. It literally didn't make sense. *But I am living here in the United States. What is this talk about citizenship in a place that I cannot get stamped into my passport and if I am not of this world, what am I? An alien?* But as I sat on my computer chair, miles and miles, days and days away from where and when this video was launched, I knew this woman's citizenship was not in North Korea. I knew that she was simply stuck in this world but her soul was not of it. She yearned for a place this world could not offer. She was looking for somewhere safe to call home and I was so confident in this moment that she could not have been the only one in search of this. For once in my life, I think I understood very clearly what I thought was once bologna.

***

If anyone were to have asked me what I wanted to do in that moment, it would have been to tell as many people I could about Jesus. It was when I began to write this book. Because I knew that my safe place to call home was with Him. I could not tell you the last time I found myself lost or shaken about the circumstances that this world would hold me captive in, because I know where I am going when I'm gone. It's not to say that I'm perfect, because God knows I'm the least of the sort. It is to say that I am confident in the One who makes it perfect, even when it hurts.

It physically pained my insides to think that there were so many others like this woman who were at a loss of identity and in need of comfort. It killed me to know that I was allowing myself to let this kind of tragedy endure while sitting comfortably and editing some photos while people were seriously struggling out there. The term *refuge* in itself means a place of protection and shelter, a safe haven, a form of relief in times of trouble. This woman on my computer screen was no refugee; she was still just as lost as so many of us. She didn't need another country to place an identity with. She needed Jesus.

I thought about her specific story and how she found herself there. My heart broke when thinking about how long I have danced around the problem going on in North Korea and how much I spewed apathy back in its face. I began to think about the current leader of North Korea and the suffering he was causing to his people with or without knowing it. Then I began to just think about him. Undoubtedly, he seemed to be one of the most hated people in this world. I looked up some photos of him online and just stared. At first, I looked at them with a bitter heart because I placed my blame for this woman's circumstances on him. Then I looked again.

He was just another person. No stronger, weaker, more or less a person than me. I wondered what got him there and what his own troubles were. I wondered if he's ever heard about Jesus. I wondered if he had ever been given a real opportunity to be loved.

My heart wasn't so bitter anymore because I couldn't help but think that if someone had witnessed true love in his or her lifetime, the individual could not be doing what this guy was doing today. Something told me that he had never been truly loved with the kind of love I receive everyday from my awesome friends and family around me and it was then when I felt so deeply sorry for him, this deep and agonizing form of sorrow. I began to look at the photos of the guy with a heart of love and I realized it wasn't this poor guy to blame; it was this broken world that he just happened to stumble upon.

He was the stem of such chaos, but he was not the root. The root of it all was that we're all born into our own lines of trials. We, by nature, will carry our separate burdens from the day we first breathe air. And regardless of what others tell you, none are more or less significant. We will all struggle with these issues that are each to our own, but the beauty of it is that in the struggle we can bond and unite. The struggle in itself is universal and real. The struggle in itself is the devil wanting to win our hearts over because he wants us to believe we are the only ones who face them. But that is a complete lie. We all have the capabilities to feel for one another. It's not a war between countries and people. It's a war between heaven and hell.

The North Korean leader's struggle was not so foreign to me after all. His story revolved around the loss of identity. A wonder of self-worth. The confusion of purpose and truth. He was just as lost as the refugee. He was just as lost as me not too long ago. He was just another person, hoping to make it right in this world.

Before I knew it, I found myself praying for him. I hoped the same for him as I did for the refugee; that he would be found and that he would stop looking in all of the wrong places. And in my brilliantly tragic Korean writing skills, I decided to write him a letter. Is that crazy? Probably. But indeed I wrote him a letter that day and said if he needed someone to call, I would be there. I didn't agree with anything he was doing, but I told him that if he ever needed someone to talk to, I'd listen. I wouldn't be one to judge, but to simply be, because that's what Jesus did for me.

I sent the letter to an address I found after a brief research and I don't really know what happened to it. Maybe that letter was confiscated and burnt. Maybe it didn't even leave the States. Perhaps it was sitting on the his desk under a pile of other things he never plans to touch. I don't know. But at least I have made it clear to let myself know that I don't fear people. Nor do I hate them. Any of them. We are all born into this world into specific stories and are often held captive of its particular culture. I cannot be so quick to blame individuals for the ways in which they act when I have done so little to take the time to listen to their history and their beginning. I believe if we start looking at people as just people…people like you and me…it would be ridiculously hard to simply hate them. It would rather be a form of mourning we would feel for others. To know that someone else cannot and will not choose to understand the deeper meanings of living and being is tragic and something we ought to live our lives to change. I choose to recognize people as people and carry hope for them when they cannot for themselves. I believe this is the way we can and will change the world.

Fearlessly.

Lovingly.

Unconditionally.

I believe we can change the world with love.

***

In college, I was a friend with someone who competed in the Miss America pageants. I remember once we watching her competitors' responses to the various questions that would be asked. I laughed out loud when one simply replied, "World peace," to the question, "If you could have one thing in this world, anything, what would it be?"

I guess I laughed because it was such a typical and artificial thing to say. I also laughed because I had always assumed it to be impossible. I was very wrong. I was very immature in my faith. Not to say that I am ever done growing and not to say I am no longer immature in my ways, but have at least come to have hope. I think we believe change is impossible because we don't go about it with the mindset that people are all just people. We place people in our minds with labels of countries and stereotypes and stigmas. We look at the world as a broken thing and we don't look at the individuals who can change it. We go in so hopeless and faithless about the world, giving the ones we are familiar with a benefit of the doubt, while giving others skepticism and a lack to understand.

When we try to produce change, we should not be surprised that our works alone were insufficient. Because it wasn't ever the work that changed the world, it was the heart behind the work. If the latent reason behind why we want to change people or the world is because of the need to show that we are right or because we actually hate them, it will never work. People will not be moved or compelled to make a difference because hate has always been so common. Hate is produced everywhere. But what if we tried to change the world with love? To see something so different, so rare and unique, something worthwhile to stop and gaze upon because one might be curious as to when he or she will see it again.

Yes, it might look crazy. And yes, we certainly might not get "our way". It might even hurt and be completely ridiculed upon. But if our way was simply to love and our mission was that in itself, then something tells me the victory was ours from the beginning. Something tells me we would shock, move, and compel the world to cause more change than anything else we can fathom because people are people. And people are made in such ways to love.

People are attracted to love, and like we have gone over, love changes people. Even those we least expect.

I have learned that when the loving gets hard, it is that the opposite party is unable to receive such a thing, it is usually me denying them of the opportunity.

Chapter Thirteen:

My Tattoo Doctor

I went in to get my second tattoo a few months ago at a place a few blocks down from my house. I had scribbled the verse from the Bible that reads: "It always protects, it always trusts, it always hopes, it always perseveres," from 1 Corinthians, chapter thirteen, verse seven, on a ripped piece of napkin from my flight back from Newark, New Jersey years ago. It meant something so dear and special to me for the sake of the moment when I wrote it and on this Saturday morning, I felt so compelled to march on over to the nearest tattoo parlor to get it inked on my right shoulder blade.

The place was called Love Tattoo. It was quiet and humble from the outside. I had driven past this place all of the previous times I had seen it and it never occurred to me just how curious its name was. As I approached the entrance, I noticed the open sign was turned off. I peeked inside and tried yanking on the door. To my surprise, it was open and I almost pulled the handle off as I proceeded to fall backwards.

There was a man covered in tattoos standing inside with a bunch of pencils in his hands, trying not to laugh.

"Oh hello!" I shouted, "I wasn't sure if you guys were open!"

The man was tall and had glasses like my stepfather. He peered over at his dark open sign. With a few cuss words and a generous welcome, he informed me that he was running late all morning and promised it'd never happen again. I wasn't quite sure if I was planning on getting any more tattoos in the future, let alone at this specific shop, but something made me believe his promise. He said his name was Dave and that he was glad to see me. I thanked him for his hospitality and told him what I wanted. Within moments of signing a few sheets of paper and fidgeting with my crumpled piece of napkin, Dave escorted me into his office.

As I entered, the first thing I noticed was the Nintendo-64 game system installed to his huge plasma television to the left. The television itself was playing one of the Star Wars films while his shelves were lined with action figures and old books. The floor was spotless and his cupboards were made of cherry wood. There was a beautiful piece of painting hanging above his leather couch and his work desk reminded me of the one inside my English professor's office. An aroma of brown sugar and vanilla captivated my senses as I just stood there astounded and a bit confused.

As Dave approached my back with the tattoo needles in his hands, I asked him about the random things I would see around his office. To my surprise, he had a very specific purpose and reason for all of the things inside, even down to the Star Wars movie playing quietly over in the corner. It was all to benefit the comfort and ease of the clients and to create an atmosphere to optimize his practice of being a tattoo artist. I felt like I was dreaming. His office should have been on a set for some movie with Tom Hanks playing the role of Dave himself.

"So did you always know this was what you wanted to do?"

He snickered and spoke sarcastically, "Yeah because we all grow up aspiring to be a sketchy tattoo artist, right?"

I smiled at his humor as I watched Luke Skywalker soaring across the television screen and waited. I could feel him slowing down his needlework on my back and he spoke again.

"You'll laugh. I was actually a pre-med student over at Grand Valley State University way back when."

"Oh yeah?" I said.

"Yeah. This dude right here could have been your doctor. Isn't that a wonder to think about?"

"What made you change your mind?" I asked.

"I hope you don't misunderstand," Dave began to say, "But I realized there was something distinctly different between me and my fellow nursing and pre-med students."

I entertained thoughts about my tattoo artist Dave sitting in his studded leather jacket amongst a lecture hall filled with blindingly white coats.

Dave continued, "They cared about people. You know? To the point of affection. I'd overhear tearful conversations about how one of the nursing students witnessed a loss of a lung cancer patient or how so-and-so would stay after his scheduled hours because he wanted to give a dying guy some extra company. And Ji, one day it just hit me that I didn't care about these people like the way my classmates did. Sounds harsh, but it was the truth. I see what you're getting inked on your back, and I gotta salute you for that because I can't love so easily. I wanted to become a surgeon because I was competent, capable, and had the steady hands for it. I didn't care about most of the patients I would have to work with in my internships because, to be honest with you, it drove me nuts when I would hear their stories. So many of them got to where they were in their health because of something they could have prevented or controlled in the past. But they didn't care to do so because they knew they'd be covered on our Medicare and Medicaid while there are actually desperate people in other worlds who are far more qualified, in my opinion, for urgent care than these McDonald's addicts and smokers."

This guy Dave was giving me more to think about than I ever thought I would while getting a tattoo. And it had nothing to do with the permanent infliction I was causing on my body. We were about halfway done with the first line of the Scripture at this point and Dave was dabbing on some extra ointment for good measure. It felt cool and relieving.

"Wow, well I appreciate your honesty, Dave. Thanks for sharing that," I said, "So how did you end up as a tattoo artist?"

Dave began tattooing again, "Well like any college student, I needed to go find some work to make end's meat while taking classes. And I just happened to find a job at a nearby tattoo parlor. Funny how things like that work out. I did their paperwork and the financial calculations for their practice. I thought the people who would come in had some awesome backgrounds to share and I started picking up the artistic end of it. Conveniently, this was all happening right around the time I started losing passion for med school. Looking back, I don't think I ever had passion for it. And in the meantime, this new gig totally fit what my heart was looking for."

"What *was* your heart looking for, Dave?" I wasn't sure if this was the kind of normal talk people had with their tattoo artists. I wasn't sure if people spoke at all. But we somehow managed to find ourselves here and I was starting to adore it.

Dave let out a sigh. It wasn't the kind of sigh that sounded like a drag. It was an alleviating sigh that comes out of wholly content people, "You know, Ji. I think I was looking for smart and selfless human beings. See, because here at a tattoo parlor, people know exactly what they are getting themselves into and the reasons for why they want it. Maybe that isn't the case for every tattoo shop in the world. But I make sure that is how my business is run here at Love Tattoo. How many times did I ask you if you were certain about your tattoo design before we came into my office, Ji?"

"Like, a lot. At least seven times." It was true. He asked me to the point where I wondered if he thought I was kidding.

"Exactly. You had multiple chances to back out. But I made sure that you had a clear conscience of how and why you wanted to do something irreversible to your body. And you had a pretty legit reason. You had thought deep about it. And you're smart. You were selfless because you weren't just wasting my time or anyone else's money. You're the kind of clients I like. You're the kind of 'patients' I prefer, if you will. I think I was looking for work where I would find myself surrounded by people who could make me a better person and allow me to feel like my service wasn't done in vain. And I found it here more than in my pre-med courses or while shadowing a doctor. I mean, yeah, look around my office. It's not the most respectable thing…when people ask me about my occupation, I usually refer to myself as a small business owner rather than saying I tattoo people just so they don't judge me right away. I get it; it doesn't hold the best reputation. But the thing is, I know that I am a far better version of who I could be here rather than having been a rich surgeon without a care for the thing I did because my heart was still searching. Am I making sense? I feel like I'm rambling."

He was. He was totally rambling but I was soaking it all up.

"You're making sense, Dave. I get you."

He continued, "And although I found so many of the sick and powerless patients in the hospitals to be rather thoughtless and selfish, they were still people too, you know? And people deserve to be taken care of by others who care. I knew I couldn't provide that, and that wasn't fair to them. No way."

***

Dave doesn't know this, but he was one of the coolest guys I had ever met. If I could have tipped him the entirety of my tattoo cost itself, I would have. It's one thing to watch people love what they do, but it's another to see their purpose and reason for loving what they do. Within my entire walk back home, I thought about what I would have done in his situation as a poor pre-med student. I thought about what my parents would have said or what my fellow colleagues would have said. Then I thought about Dave's heart and what God might think of Dave. I thought about Dave's office and how he had decided to title his practice, "Love Tattoo".

Dave mentioned over and over again how he lacked the ability to empathize and to care for other people. If I didn't know any better, I would almost say that he boasted in it. But as I slowly peeled back my bandage and moved my eyes along his beautiful artistry on my shoulder blade, I was convinced he was wrong. He cared. He cared a lot. He was one of the most empathetic and careful people I had ever met.

Now when I see tattooed people, I think about Dave and how he likes to consider those individuals to be smart and selfless. I enjoy this thought because it is so different than so many others'. It may be true for some and it certainly may be not for others. I don't know. But because of my tattoo doctor,

I have somehow found more space in my heart to not place people in boxes.

It may not make much sense, but it is so important to me now more than ever not assume the reasons, priorities, potentials, and ambitions of others without taking the time to listen. Who knows, some of the smartest and most selfless people in our world could be the very ones we have tucked away in a box years ago because of the way they initially approached us in our lives. Maybe we shouldn't have boxes at all. Just open offices with optimal atmosphere for others to be welcomed in.

Chapter Fourteen:

Living Miracles

In my parent's miracle of a house, there is no secure concept of privacy. In the corner of the basement where my bedroom from high school is located, one can literally hear everything. It is as though somehow the vents have been mastered to pool all noise created in the house to that specific location. To me, it was always kind of cozy this way. As borderline-creepy as this was, I liked it because everything seemed near. Everything seemed certain. To me, it was home and it was good.

The last time I visited, I stayed back inside my old room in the basement for the sake of memories as well as hearing the magical and amusing sounds of home all over again. On the first morning, I could distinctly hear little footsteps coming down the stairs. This was partially due to the fact that the noise was most definitely penetrating through the walls but it didn't help that I was also the world's lightest sleeper. And if you know your people well, you know the way in which they walk. With that being said, I could tell it was my mother coming down the stairs, but her pace was unfamiliar. It was slow, unpredictable, and so, so quiet. She was supposed to be at her housekeeping job already and I quickly became confused as to why she was still home. I simply stayed in my bed and waited for further noise.

She was soon on the other side of my door. I could hear whimpering. My mother never whimpers. My mother hardly cries.

I quickly made my way to the door and slowly opened it toward the hallway to see my precious, small mother in tears. This was as shocking as it was sobering. She had crumpled tissues in her hands and her eyes were incredibly sad.

"I'm struggling right now," she said.

Words I had never heard.

"What's wrong, mom?"

"I just got news that..." her lips were quivering so badly that she found it difficult to finish her words, "...my mama collapsed this morning, and I can't be there for her."

Our grandmother was still in South Korea. Although my mother is one of seven children, she was the second youngest and the only daughter who stayed back to take care of her elderly mother when all of my aunts and uncles went on to school and other endeavors. When my mother was remarried to my stepfather over fifteen years ago, I recall leaving my grandmother being the most difficult thing. I can still remember the grey face of my mother as we waved our last goodbye to our grandmother from the airport portal. Since then, she has always referred to my grandmother as "her mother". Very rarely did she call her my "grandmother" in front of me. When we would talk about her mother, we were still referring to her as "her mother". It was something I had always secretly appreciated. She was very dear and personal to her. She always was. And this moment, I could tell, was absolutely tragic.

"Mom, I'm so sorry," I said.

These are the moments when words will do just about nothing. I almost felt foolish for speaking in the first place. I held my mother in our hallow hallway of the basement as she cried long on my shoulder.

"But mom," I finally said again, "She has lived an incredibly blessed and long life, won't you agree? Most people don't get that. This is life. She is aging and this isn't awful. This is nature and it's beautiful. What a great thing it is to know she is still breathing and here with us. She still has time to—"

"But she's not. She's so far away. I'm so far away."

"Mom. There are people taking care of her. It's okay."

"It's not that. I don't care about that. I'm not crying about that."

I kept staring into her wet eyes.

"She doesn't know God."

Quiet.

"I need to tell her about God, Who can save her, before she leaves this place. She needs to know about God. Before it's too late and—"

My mother wept so hard. This was someone's daughter and she was crying for her mother for the first time in fifteen years. And I realized why she was crying. Her mother's life was on the line. Not the kind of life we live here on earth, but the only one that really matters. The kind she and I both stumbled upon when moving to the United States and meeting Grace. As I cradled my mother and she sat still her in her housekeeping uniform, I flashed back to every role I had ever seen this woman play in my life.

An independent mother of one.

A "successful" businesswoman.

A popular elitist of the block.

A carefree travel agent.

A remarried entrepreneur.

An oblivious immigrant.

An unforeseen dry cleaning lady.

A tired mother of two.

A sudden churchgoer.

A host mother for the needy.

A stationed missionary.

A willful housekeeper.

A tearful, hurt, and woeful daughter.

Today, she was not an underappreciated, mocked, anonymous foreign housekeeper cleaning up for some drunken teenagers in a dark and dirty hotel room in downtown Grand Rapids. She was my hero. She had been risking her life and sanity for mine since we first stepped off that plane with our two duffle bags and a pocket of change. And as weak as she may have felt, I had never seen her stronger.

Outside of our window, clouds were shamelessly passing by. Their shadows casted patterns inside the room in a comfortable manner as time in itself seemed to be on standby for us, for once.

"Thank you, Ji-Hyun," my mother finally said, "Although it hurts, it is nice to know you're by my side. Thank you for never leaving my side."

These were words I didn't deserve.

And In that moment, we were there for each other. This was family. This was God continuously answering my childlike prayer from when my relationship with Him first began. Because of God, we were still together. Because of God, my mother so desperately yearned to be with her own mother. God was constantly gluing our concept of family back together in the cleverest of ways. In fifteen years or in just the passing of just moments, He was never done working. He was always there.

***

My mother walked back upstairs after an hour or two and I slowly closed the door behind her. I sat back down on the edge of my bed and stayed there halfheartedly. I wanted to give her a way. I knew there was one; but I didn't want to admit it.

I was well aware of the costs of giving her the literal once-in-a-lifetime opportunity before my grandmother passed away. I was also well aware that she had no money or time. The only way to pay for the expenses was to use the money I had saved up to publish this book. I was also conveniently back in town so I could fill in for her various duties while she was gone. It was a sporadic and urgent idea but I knew it could work. The amount in my savings was ridiculously close to what was necessary for this specific situation and I couldn't think all of this was coincidence. It never is. Coincidence is a word for the faithless.

I asked some of my closest friends to pray with me as I mustered up the prudence to be well discerned in what I did. They were passionate, heartfelt, and absolutely sincere in their agreement to do so. I also called my stepfather to let him know my plans, and these were his words,

"You show me love like I have never seen. I'm sorry for being insufficient in more ways than one. But thank you for trusting the One who is more than sufficient. Thank you for not leaning on me and your mother to learn the things that are truly important in this life."

This was the longest sentence he had ever spoken to me in all of my life spent with him. He will also never know what these words meant to me.

And so I did it. A few hours passed and I bought my mother a ticket for the next available opening. At first, it felt kind of crazy. But then I thought about it and it wasn't long before I realized how crazy it would have been if I hadn't.

This was exactly the kind of stuff I was writing about in here and yet there I was, potentially wasting an opportunity for God to be glorified because of my selfish endeavors. We so often walk around in circles like that because the devil tries so hard to weasel back inside our tender hearts. But our God is better than that. Our God is stronger than that.

To use my measly words to describe my mother's reaction when I told her would be a huge understatement. She was so quiet but her heart was loud with utter joy and disbelief. She then said she felt horribly sick when realizing it meant I would have to set back my personal dreams. But I told her she was hurting my feelings if she continued to feel that way, because it was true. She wasn't accepting a gift I willfully wanted to give. It was in the sacrifice that was worth it.

As I watched her shake and rejoice like a child on Christmas day, I was able to have the tiniest glimpse of why God does the things He does for us. I think I could understand why He would give His one and only Son, Jesus, and sacrifice Him for the sake of those He loves. I realize that this metaphor is hardly such its case. But it's in these momentary breaths of life where we are able to connect the dots and see that He is the real deal. This kind of love is, indeed, crazy. But it is most certainly the cream of the crop. Once we taste it, we can never go back.

The rest of that night was as weird as any. You see, once you have accepted God into your life, you would understand this well. There is no such thing as a boring or an ordinary day when in the midst of God. I sat back down on the edge of my bed and bowed my head in prayer. I didn't really know what to do at this point and although I was beyond ecstatic for my mother, I didn't know what it meant for me in order to make this book into print. And through praying, I realized that money is not a stumbling block for God. It never was and it wasn't going to be now. My heart was reassured and I knew in His time, His will would happen. I was content with not knowing and I was content that He would still have me. The minute I opened my eyes, I received a message from one of the friends I had contacted earlier that day. She had collected enough money in that time span to reimburse the all of the expenses in full.

Finding myself in absolute awe, I was hesitant to receive such a gift. Then I remembered what I had told my mother. By receiving, I was accepting a gift that was willfully given. I was inviting others into the ministry of love and allowing them to see the smallest glimpse of God's heart. It was in my part to expose it to others. It was simply too good to keep hidden, so I didn't.

***

In just the next morning, my mother and I made a little road trip to Chicago's international airport and before I knew it, I was waving goodbye to a daughter who would soon be united with her dearly missed mother. This face was one so different than the one I could remember from fifteen years ago. This was a face that had discovered joy and love. This was a face that knew God and was ready to share His embrace. This was the closing of one chapter and the opening of what was next.

***

My mother tried to connect with me the next day. I had missed the call but my phone has forever saved this message, "I got to hold my mama's hand and pray with her for the first time today. She didn't want to accept it at first but she was willing. I have prayed for this moment for as long as I can remember. You know this well. I never thought it'd be possible. Thank you for holding my hand and praying with me all these years, Ji-Hyun, even when I didn't want to accept. Though you never showed it, I know you have been praying for me years beyond my apprehension. I could feel it. Thank you for waiting for me. Thank you for believing in me even when I made things seem impossible. Thank you for holding God's hand and taking all of us with you. You mended hearts that have been born so broken. Remember to thank God, Ji-Hyun, because He, indeed, is a God who overcomes the impossible. We are living out what was impossible yesterday, my daughter. We are living miracles."

Redeeming love.

***

Looking back, there is not much I can deny in regards to God. It was always prayer that got us through. It was always prayer that saved us. These prayers allowed our hearts to see. We were able to finally see that miracles are everywhere, waiting to be noticed. And God is forever amongst us, waiting for us to receive His crazy love and to be welcomed in.

A few days ago, I made myself trek back to Hope College and visit the Campus Ministries office. I got on my knees in the lobby. It was early in the morning and the sun was whispering his good-mornings to the world. I looked upon the wooden cross, the same cross I walked away from years ago.

I did not find myself counting the hours of my days anymore. What mattered was right now. What mattered was right here.

I looked across the room and there stood the wooden cross exactly where I last found it. Leaning purposefully against the wall. I think there is a Father in heaven. And perhaps He has always been near. I was beginning to see the lines on His face. I no longer aimed to see His knees or

His ankles. I think I had been wrong about His black socks the entire time. He spoke things like, "Ji, yes. It's okay. It's alright. I'm here. Look. Come to me!" And I believed Him. I knew His voice well. Everything was okay, indeed. And He was only drawing me closer.

Chapter Fifteen:
Finding Stars

It has been a wish of mine to be able to see every state in this beautiful country. Recently, Virginia—along with all of the states in between there and Michigan—has been crossed off of the bucket list. I had very little idea of where I was headed and who I was with, but to this day it remains to be one of my favorite experiences thus far.

Near where I live is this narrow overpass where car accidents frequently occur due to the way it is designed. As a driver, you cannot see what is coming up ahead when traveling under it and so I always caution my friends to pay close attention when taking the roads to my house. On this particular evening, I found myself using my sweet time heading back home. It was that awkward time of the night where it was too late to really embark on a new adventure with friends but it was still too early for me to want to call it a day. As I was about to maneuver through the accident-prone region, I noticed a silhouette of a person standing against one of the columns beneath the overpass.

My initial plan was to continue driving. But as I approached the figure, I noticed it was a woman who looked to be in her early thirties. She had a medium-sized bag slung heavy over her shoulder but her stumbling caused me to believe it was not just the bag that made her walking seem inadequate.

As my Volkswagen shamelessly crunched over every pebble on the curb while nearing the woman, she flinched and fell backwards, barely catching herself with her limp arms. *Oh boy,* I thought, *there's no way she's going home alone.* I walked out of my car and offered a hand. To this gesture, she stared at my limb hanging before me and murmured something beneath her breath.

I smiled discreetly and kept my hand out.

"I'm sorry, what was that? Could I help you?"

The woman smirked sharply and finally looked me in the eyes. She had beautiful eyes. She had a lovely smile. But it was so thickly covered by her tiredness and makeup; I was unsure of its sincerity. She spoke but her words remained few, "I said... What. Is. The. Point."

She then licked her lips and pulled out a cigarette. I looked around casually and could feel the passerby's staring. She was sitting in her sequined skirt in such a way where her bare butt was visibly touching the cold gravel. As I bent down to make her body less visible to the road, a blue hatchback drove by with three guys hollering from the window.

"Hey sexy!"

"You want a ride with me?"

"We'll take you home tonight!"

Their foul laughter sounded like hyenas and it echoed nauseatingly throughout the columns. My heart cringed.

I picked up her bag and walked to the passenger side of my car. There are moments in life when it becomes clear to us that, by nature, we are all pretty similar. Regardless of history or circumstance, we are all just supposed to be there for each other. There seems to be a protective instinct of knowing that we are no more or less human than one another. This reality in itself should rest assure a heart can hear when another heart is yearning for something. She took the hint and picked herself up from the ground. As I kept the passenger door open, she crawled inside. I popped open my trunk and placed her bag next to my art supplies and slammed it shut for it was about to be quite the ride.

At this point, I didn't really know what I was doing. I started driving around the block and watched the darkness of the night settle in completely. Looking over to my newfound passenger, I couldn't help but taste the apathy that reeked from her posture. She didn't care who I was, where we were headed, or what tomorrow would look like. Her eyes were lingering at the sky as the stars reflected in her distinctly blue irises.

"The night sky is my favorite," I began to say. She continued setting her gaze toward the heavens but I knew she was listening.

"I like the stars because it makes me feel like there is something bigger going on than me. I like it because it makes life a mystery."

"Am I a mystery to you?" she aptly responded.

It took me a moment to answer her. I had multiple responses running through my head. Of course she was a mystery to me. I had no idea where she came from or who she was. Yet, she wasn't a mystery at all. She reminded me of some of my closest friends in ways I couldn't describe. She also reminded me of myself.

"Can I ask where we are going?" I said.

"Well I don't know about you but I need to go to Fairfax."

"...As in Fairfax, *Virginia*?"

My tired friend looked away from the sky and picked at her nails. They were vibrant and gold as they shimmered like the stars eavesdropping from above.

Up ahead was a vacant parking lot of where an old Target store used to be. I pulled in slowly and parked the car near the dimly lit sign.

"Well, thanks for the ride!" she laughed menacingly as she began to reach for the door.

"What? No. Wait, please talk to me." I lost my touch of what was considered socially acceptable at the moment and grabbed her left wrist. It was cold outside and if anything, I took her further north by a mile or two rather than toward Virginia.

"Why do you care?" she stammered while shaking off my grip from her tangled bracelets.

"I don't have to if you don't want me to," I replied.

That was not the response she was expecting. I could tell because her eyebrows rose as she looked to the ground and bit her lower lip. It might sound crazy, but the longer I spent time with this woman, the more I could not help but care about where she was going. This idea of not wanting to admit she needed something was a trick I was very familiar with. This was how I lived most of my life. Our kind like to be chased after and confirmed that people are watching and concerned and yet somehow play it off as though we don't have a care in the world because we need to feel independent. But we are oftentimes the most dependent of all; so dependent that we can't seek help on our own.

"Do you need a ride to Fairfax?" I asked.

She didn't speak. She just kept staring at the ground and fidgeting with her fingers. It was nearing ten o' clock by this time and I could feel her soberness kicking in.

"Tell me you need a ride to Fairfax," I said in a more demanding tone.

Still quiet. Still adrift.

I began to turn my car back on and I pretended to reach over toward her door handle.

"Okay, fine!" she blurted.

"Well okay then," I said and I took out my rugged GPS from the glove compartment. Did I feel kind of nuts? Oh heck yeah. Did I have a clue as to what I was in for? Nope. But I remembered all of the times people have stepped into my life with no agenda or invitation. I thought about my best friend from high school and how she left me a voicemail in the darkest hour of my life...how all it takes to make a difference sometimes is to be fully present. I was looking for something to do that night. Here it was. I was going on a road trip with a woman with golden nails.

It was not until two hours later that she began to talk. This was mainly because she had to use the restroom while I was the owner of the world's most controlled bladder. After our brief rest stop, she began to tell me bits and pieces of her day and how she ended up on the side of the street. Turns out, she was up in Michigan visiting her girlfriend for the week and she had just been dumped. I listened intently as we cruised seamlessly into the night and it became clearer to me that this woman and I were not so different from each other. Other than looks, sexual orientation, and sizes of bladders, we were pretty open and honest about what we were aiming for in life and we both didn't take break ups well.

"I'm Ji, by the way," I said as we were entering Ohio, "it's pronounced like the letter."

"I ain't tellin' you my name if that's what you're thinking."

"Oh, that's fine."

There was stillness in the air.

"I guess you can call me Star, though," she chuckled, "You says you like the stars? 'Cuz they're mysterious? I like to be mysterious."

Star made a great travel partner. She carried conversations but it would be made obvious when she lost interest. She didn't fake much. Being quiet was okay and she was not shy to take on the role of being the DJ.

She licked her lips again, "do you smoke?"

"Smoke what?"

I didn't know why I answered like that. I had never smoked anything in my life.

She pulled out another cigarette from her jean jacket and offered one to me. I shook my head as I kept my eyes on the road and she let out one of her many laughs.

"You don't smoke nothin'?"

"No."

"What about like the good stuff?"

I looked toward her and smiled, "No, not even the good stuff."

"You, like, against all that?"

"It's a personal choice I had made a long time ago."

"Oh I see. You like a Christian or somethin'?"

I noticed Star was eying the turquoise cross that was dangling above my dashboard.

"I believe in Jesus, yes," I replied.

"So is that why you won't smoke?"

To this day, this was probably one of the most refreshing moments of my life. I have never met someone so honest about his or her questions on my beliefs.

I looked at her again and responded, "Well, can I ask why you *do* smoke?"

"Sure. It feels good. It's better than life."

"I guess I already feel pretty good, Star. For me, Jesus is better than life."

"So, you high off of Jesus?"

We both laughed. Star was giggling so hard that she was keeling over with her hair flowing freely out the window. I kept giggling too; *this woman thinks I'm crazy.*

"I didn't always feel so good though, Star. I hope you don't think I have always been clean. I've been drunk before.

When I was seventeen and I did it to impress my boyfriend at the time. I've also nearly overdosed by choice. I've been very dark. I've had my days. I guess I just chose different marbles to play with."

"How old are you now?"

"Twenty-one."

"You know, for a Christian, you're pretty screwed up, too."

I grinned one of my biggest grins, "I know I am, Star. That's why I need Jesus. I'm just someone who woke up one day and realized I can't do this life on my own and maybe there's a reason for that. You think I'm messed up? Well, you're preaching to the choir."

Star just stared at me.

***

The rest of the drive consisted of a few detours, several boxes of Crackerjacks, and a little bit of snoring on her part. She gave me assurance on the hopes I had for my future and I told her that she would do just fine without her ex-girlfriend. She talked to me about her thoughts on religion and politics and the conversation was the most applicable and helpful lesson I have ever received. She was raw, blunt, honest, and real. I gave her some insight on my knowledge and apprehension of smoking. Later, she revealed to me that she has had the same suicide story during her high school days. I told her about how I want to find my biological father one day and she said she'd be down to join. I didn't know her name but I guess she was willing to stand by my side.

When we arrived to Fairfax, it was around eight in the morning of the next day. Star was asleep next to me with dried mascara all around her face and I found myself parked in the parking lot of a Target store yet again.

While waking Star up, I noticed a large tattoo on her right shoulder. It had been covered all throughout the drive because of her jean jacket. From the looks of it, it hadn't been touched up in a while but I could still make it out clearly,

"In Christ alone,
my hope is found."

She woke up and I simply saw her for who she was.

***

As much as I choose to believe that stars are but miracles intricately and purposefully placed in the sky by God on high, I also choose to believe that Star is also one of those many miracles. Maybe I will never see her again, or maybe she will be at the same restaurant as me tonight as I write this from a bench in Chicago. I am never too certain on how God sets the stage. But I do know this: miracles are all around, waiting to be noticed. From what I can tell, people like Star are just as intricately and purposefully placed in our lives by God on high. And much like the stars in the night sky, miracles are always there, regardless of the condition of the climate or amount of fog before our eyes. I suppose it is up to us whether or not we want to trust they exist and to see the glory of their sheer beauty.

Chapter Sixteen:

Amazing Grace

Can I confess something? I didn't really know how to start this chapter. I knew I wanted to talk more on grace, but how does one really go about starting that? Grace, to me, is such an ungraspable concept that even if I gathered all of the stories in the world about grace and compile them into one mega-story, it would still be short of the much glory it deserves. When writing this chapter, I wanted to work on it in a place where I could find tranquility because this is not a topic I take lightly. I did not want distractions, nor did I want to waste time.

It was a Sunday afternoon and I was on Hope's campus. Some students were moseying back from church services while the rest were just getting up to touch their homework for the first time in the weekend. What this meant for me was that I needed to be wise and selective in which coffee shop to settle in because nine out of the ten would be chaotic with procrastination stations and flying paper everywhere.

I settled with a coffee shop just off of the freeway; it was the one most out of reach. I saw its entrance sign straight ahead to the right. It was also then when I noticed that I happened to be backed up in the left lane and it also was Michigan's seemingly one and only left *turn* lane. If you are not familiar with Michigan, let me enlighten you and say that there are no such things as left turns. Or so I thought. I guess this rule applied for everywhere in Michigan but here.

Immersed within traffic of people who needed to get to their own line of destination, I made a bold move and flicked on the right blinker. There was no way anyone to my right would let me in. This was out of my personality. I usually prefer not to make it frustrating or difficult for others while driving (secretly because I am afraid to get flipped off or honked at) and I would much rather take the safe option of making a loop around. But I was being brave this day. I needed to get to this coffee shop and get to work. I needed to keep all the ideas I had about the concept of grace in my head and type them into my computer before they slipped away.

Sure enough, there were the intense starers and flat-mouthed head-shakers judging my driving technique and lack of preparation and aim. It was fine. I deserved it. And of course, the moment I slyly slipped into the right lane, I made it just in time to be greeted by another red light. Stopped again. Slowed once more.

Maybe the loop-around would have been quicker. I did not know. I also did not know how much time I had wasted by trying to be efficient in choosing this coffee shop. What I did know, however, was that there was now a beggar standing to the right of my car. We could have all kept pretending that I was so focused on my end goal with my eyes straight forward as I diligently waited upon the light to turn green. But we also know that was a joke. Failing such endeavor was why I ended up here in the first place.

He was looking at me. I just knew it. If it was not my keen peripherals that made this obvious, it was definitely the fact that I was less than seven feet away from him, sitting comfortably on the other side of my car door. Even if he were blind, he could have smelled my sweaty guilt from the distance between us.

I was gut-checked.

I was also curious.

In an ever so casual manner of pretending to grab something from the passenger's seat, I glanced up and over. He was a man who looked to be in his mid-forties. Now we were both very much aware we saw each other. He was standing coldly on the side of the street with a sign in his hand. It read:

> *"Single Father.*
> *In Desperate Need.*
> *Anything Helps.*
> *Even Prayer."*

At the bottom of the sign was an ichthys. A Jesus fish.

No, not me. God, you have other people You can use.

There are people who throw money bills all around for kicks. I knew this to be fact; I was a friend to many of them. This five-dollar bill in my wallet was literally all I had at the moment. I was a broke twenty-one-year-old fresh out of college and this stipend was going to get me my next coffee at the shop I should already be at by this point. I was supposed to be writing about grace right now. This was not my responsibility. This was not my moment.

Maybe all of that was true. But so was this: I was not a single parent. I was not presently hungry. I was not freezing outside, nor was I in desperate need to put food into my children's mouths. I did not have people dependent on me whom are probably waiting at home, hoping to some greater being that they will not have to fall asleep with their little stomachs eating themselves up that night. I was not struggling right now. But my neighbor was.

What if he was lying?

What if he was what we all assume of people who take other's money? What were his true intentions? Was he sober? Did he even have children? Could he attack me? Was that sloppy sketch of the Jesus fish purely bait for suckers like me? Will he want more? Why is he not out finding a job instead? How did he afford that haircut? Where did he get that North Face jacket he was wearing?

Did it matter?

I had to really ask myself: Are my actions dependent on whether or not someone is being truthful with me or are they dependent on who I say I am and Who I stand for? If it is the former, who is the real liar here?

Jesus gave me His everything. This much, I was assured of. Yet I could not give Him and His people five dollars because to me, this was my everything in my tiny little perspective of *world* at the moment.

I was there. This was my responsibility. This was my moment, because it was obviously already happening before me. Do we find these seemingly harmless moments of interference and interactions with humanity to be mere coincidence? Are they only considered to be profound and "by the grace of God" if they seem to cause good fruit for own personal benefit? What if it was a possibility that every breath we take on its own is each their divine appointment? What if the concept of free will simply exists so that we may desire to seek His beauty in the moment? What if it were true that everything happening, even now—as big, as boring, as normal, or as different as they are—is *all* by the grace of God and it is not His fault if we fail to open our hearts to this radical truth?

In times like these when we make eye contact with a situation at hand, things are now on our side of the ball court. They know we know. And we know we know. *But are we going to pick up the ball?* Since when did we become so apathetic to truth and so indulged in our own agenda that carries no greater importance?

When the man looked back into my eyes, it was not a face of bitterness or disbelief at the fact that I did not initiate to help. It was simply a face that was fully aware that life gets tough and he understood me no matter my lack of generosity.

You know, we often find ourselves in conversation of how no one is stepping forward to stop poverty, world hunger, bullying, communists, online hackers, human trafficking, poor fashion statements, you name it. Where were the people? Why didn't anyone see this coming? Why didn't anybody show the kids love or teach them empathy before they went and shot up a school? Who are their parents? Why aren't more people assisting in the damages of natural disasters? Why is there so much money in such tiny pockets and not enough going around?

As I continued to sit in my sweat inside my car, it hit me like an unforgiving brick wall. It hurt. I realized that I could complain all I want about how everyone in this world seems to be lacking. I could have pointed fingers at the cars in front and behind me of how no one else seems to be doing much. Cleverness is key and criticism is a sure byproduct. But this was the hitter; I am also in no place to speak at all unless I have done my part.

Oh but I am so busy? I am young? They're not my kids? They're not my problem? I have a lot going on in my job right now? In my finances right now? In my love life right now? I began to wonder, when is it ever the "right" time to do anything? Truth is, time will not slow down for us. We all know this. The needy and these moments of urgency will not purposefully sustain and wait until our preferred and ideal time of arrival. How often do we hear, "if only I had known then—", "I wish my children were still young so that—", "where did the years go and how come we still have not fixed the—"?

Maybe this was the whole point. Maybe this was what it meant to truly set our goal to do His will. It was as simple as that. We ought not fill in the blanks with our finite definition of what His plans are for us. Maybe it is happening right in front of you and me. And maybe this is the point; because tomorrow is not promised but today is certainly here, begging us to look it in the eye for once instead of exist through it.

My three-year-old self did not have the volume, the knowledge, or the experience to remedy an issue of fighting parents. To be completely honest, I did not even care because I did not understand. But my issue at hand was opening a package of grape gummies. Many times, the world will not care. And many times, we honestly do not care for the world either because we have our own things that carry importance. But regardless of all of this apathy and regardless of selfish intentions, we all know when a pin drop is loud in a cloud of noise because we are all humans born with a human heart. We still know we need help by the end of the day. We also know when others do, too. It is not about the size or the shape, the age or the circumstance. It is about the will.

I scrolled my window down and offered him my five dollars. He received it full of gratitude and mercy and I continued on my interrupted route.

Pulling into the parking lot, I reran my mental reel of what just happened. I will not lie to you, I felt very philanthropic. Knowing my situation of being self-sacrificial and doing the seemingly right thing, I actually felt really proud of myself for this good deed.

God is pleased with me, I told myself. But this was not enough. I needed further affirmation. Immediately I took out my phone to text a friend to let her know that there was a man and he needed money and I gave when others did not because my heart was listening and it was good. Maybe then later my friend and I could have gotten more coffee and talk some more about how there needed to be more people like us.

Now, at this point, my car was parked. I turned off the ignition and I, again, ran the freshest batch of my mental reel of the thoughts I had told myself within the past twelve seconds.

I don't know about you, but many times I feel as though I have multiple versions of me bickering at one another and deciphering which is the real deal. As I evaluated my intentions and purpose for my behavior and goodness, I was embarrassed. Shocked in the eyes and red in the face. I put my phone back down and stared at the ceiling of my car. I was just as complacent and numb in the heart as the drivers in the cars that were in the line of traffic with me. I was no better. It wasn't about what I did; it was about the reasons why. And my reason for helping this man was pathetic. I wasn't sure if I really helped him at all. I gave to the man because I loved myself and who I was. I loved my seemingly affectionate heart and I loved that I could show it off. I didn't give because I loved God and His people. In the end, I wanted the glorification and credit. It was all intended to come back to me. It was as though I was a marble spinning round and around the inner linings of a funnel and the moment I did not actively work at keeping this perfect ratio of speed and force, I would slip down into the dark and confusing hole of pride.

Speed, here, is humility and grace.

The driving force, then, would be love.

Humility and grace are probably the hardest lessons I have ever learned. And—as we can tell here—they are also the hardest lessons I have yet to learn, still. I won't ever conquer it. I don't think that's the point. I will forever do my best to simply be.

It was humbling, indeed, to know that as I thought I would write inside of a book about grace and humanity's need for it, I was hardly one to talk. In the midst of searching for a story to tell, God had written one for me.

Grace is what God gives us to know that we can and will get another shot. Grace is knowing that He never expects us to get it right or perfect whether it is our first time or our hundredth time. Grace was Jesus turning the other cheek when He had full power to prove Himself. Grace was this man accepting my thoughtless five dollars. Grace is the truth that there are no boundaries to which it exists.

***

I finally walked into the coffee shop and a bright piece of cardstock on the floor caught my eye. It was a punch card and it was ready for the holder to use the free punch. I looked around and sought out its owner.

This yours? No?

Hey, is this yours?

No one claimed. I was the only one in line and I was just standing there with this free punch card in my hand. I looked out through the window and I could still see where the man once stood. He was no longer there. Perhaps my five dollars was sufficient. Perhaps it wasn't. I do not know and frankly, I probably never will. But what I do know is this. Thanks to the impeccable timing of when I stepped into the coffee shop, I was able to use this punch card as my own.

I drank the biggest size of the most expensive thing there that evening...and it was worth more than my measly five dollars.

Chapter Seventeen:

Golden Pavements

I have a friend named Seth. He told me I was allowed to use him in my book under one condition: that he wore a cape. Although my story regarding Seth is real and adding a cape would make it fiction, please bear with me as I try to accommodate to both parties.

Anyway, I have a friend named Seth...who wears really cool capes[1]. He will never admit it, but he is a genius. I'm not talking about the geniuses who talk so debonair that it does you better to not engage in a conversation at all. He is a genius in his way of living. I could not tell you the last time he has bought, done, or said anything without a purpose. He has been one of those people who have helped me become a better person everyday.

For a while I gave credit to myself. But then I began to realize the reason why my interactions with Seth consistently

---

[1] Unconfirmed by his parents

followed up with outcomes of growth in my character is because he invested his time with a specific purpose. The intents and purposes were always about God, whether it was spoken or not.

In retrospect, it was God, then, who would use Seth to better me because Seth was always willing to be used by Him. It wasn't me at all, who has bettered myself while spending time with Seth. I guess it wasn't completely Seth either.

It was always God.

God made Seth a genius and a good friend.

***

My good friend, Seth, is also crazy.

The good ones always seem to be.

It was nearing one o' clock in the morning when he rang. I answered without hesitation, anticipating a prank call or a request to run to McDonald's. I was wrong in every way. There were two female voices on the other end of the line and they were both speaking Korean. It was definitely not Seth asking for a Big Mac and fries with that.

Immediately I propped up from my bed and made sure I had read the caller identification correctly. I responded back in my native language. They asked if I could come over. The two women were talking from Seth's house. Not only was I not dressed, tired, and confused, but I was also out of town. After a few more minutes of awkward laughter while being on the speakerphone, I detected Seth's voice in amongst the crowd. I then heard him speak directly at me in the background in English.

"Ji! You have to come over. C'mon. The night is so young. When else are we going to have this opportunity?"

I smirked. I could hear his cape[2] flapping as he awaited a response.

What *opportunity*, you might ask? As I have said before, Seth's purpose is always about God, whether it is spoken or not. I did not need any more information from him. If it was Seth, it was good and it was purposeful, whatever it was. There was a reason why it was one in the morning. There was a reason why he would drag me out of bed and inquire for me to take a solo road trip. There was a reason these women were over at his house and even though I had not a clue quite yet, I knew it was purposeful.

So I went.

***

As I entered Seth's house, I noticed his housemates sitting unnaturally all together in the living room with these two Korean women in business attire. They both seemed wide awake while the guys looked absolutely pathetic trying to keep their eyelids up.

The room was timid at first, but after several greetings, hugs, and a few bad jokes on my part, the ice was well broken in ten minutes. Seth informed me that these women were on a business trip through the company he works with and it was their last night staying in the United States. They had spent a vast majority of their time in their visit held under tight supervision by their bosses and this was their only opportunity to experience the culture. Their flight was at eight in the morning the following day and they were determined to utilize these next few hours staying up and experiencing an American life. I giggled as I looked around at the present situation and breathed in the ridiculousness of this spontaneous happening.

---

[2] Arms

It was a Friday night, it was beautiful outside, and us twenty- to thirty-year-olds were sitting around a snug living room past one o' clock in the morning with nothing in common except for the fact that this moment in time was holding us all together. But as I glanced over at Seth with his cape draped so effortlessly upon his broad shoulders[3], this was exactly his point.

Seth wanted these ladies to hear about God. I, too, wanted these ladies to hear about God, but I was more so just thrown into the moment that I let everyone else steer in terms of where this early morning was headed.

***

We spent a good chunk of the time getting to know one another and to become familiarized each other's personalities. Seth's housemates would constantly be captivated by my bilingual-ness while our new South Korean friends had endless questions of how I got here. Their eyes would continue to widen as I explained my past and they'd respond with things like, "I wish I had that experience!" and "Is there a program for things like that?"

Jesus, I guess.

After translating some more dialogue from one side of the room to the other and laughing at the various cultural differences, we went to get Slurpee's at the gas station and started up a bonfire around four in the morning.

Jonathan, the youngest of the house, brought out a guitar and we sat around the fire full of Slurpee and slaphappy joy. The two businesswomen were laughing as they saw fireflies

---

[3] No witnesses available to validate the occurrence of either the cape or the broad shoulders.

for the first time and before we could tell, we were friends, all of us. Everything about this moment felt right. As we looked up at the stars, one of the ladies remarked at how they never got to see stars so bright where they were from because South Korea is so enriched with the city life. I began to tell them that the night sky is my absolute favorite part of nature. I explained to my warm audience that this was because it was so humbling to know that I am a very small part of a much grander scheme. I told them it felt mysterious. I thought about Star. I wished she was there sitting around the fire with us. She would've fit in perfectly.

***

As six o' clock drew near, we offered to take our two new friends to Good Time Donuts, a 24-hour idyllic donut shop where Hope College students satisfy their untimely sugar cravings. We offered to pay and that is when one of the women pulled be off to the side.

She asked me if *this* was normal.

I asked her to please define for me what normal was.

She asked me if it was common for people to pay for others without an I-O-U status or a wage, for strangers to welcome one another into a home and not only that, but to stay over night. She questioned this concept of men and women spending a significant time together without there being scandalous activity at play, and for there to be this much fun had on a regular basis without the consumption of alcohol on a weekend such as this, particularly on a college campus.

No, this is not normal at all.
This is what Jesus would do.
This is how we live our lives.

But to explain would have taken longer than the time I had been given. It also would have taken more than just my words. These are the moments where we can only hope we've allowed God to use us as much as possible in a given circumstance and He will take care of the rest in His time.

As much as I lacked words to speak, my heart absolutely broke at the idea that I might not have been doing the best of my ability to tell her gracefully and patiently about our God, the One who had saved my life from the very beginning. I wanted her to have Him, too. I wanted her to have a personal relationship with Jesus. I so desperately wanted her to have this security of knowing she could put all of her guards down because the One who had painted this world into life also had her in the forefront of His mind.

I did not know her backstory or all of the places she had been, but I did know a few things from our conversations throughout the time spent. She had told me that she did not like her job, that she felt mistreated at work, and that she was constantly nervous about eating because of what her husband might think if she one day woke up fat. She also happened to share with me that she did not know what it meant to live a life of faith. She didn't understand it. She said to spend the evening with us was the most faithful thing she'd done in a while. I wanted to hold her and shake her with love…to express to her that these temporary worries did not matter because it was all but the process of preparing her for a better thing. What she was living was, in fact, the lessons and the "experience" she was asking me about. This was Jesus working in her life. This was a potential pivotal point. This was someone walking to her salvation. I wanted to tell her that this process in itself is living out faith. To be uncertain, but certain of the God who keeps our paths aligned. This was a life of faith. This night was a moment of faith. She was, indeed, capable of living in faith. But I just stood there, tearing up at the truth that we never have enough time to share with everyone who gets a chance to hear.

As we sunk our teeth into our donuts and further engaged in the time we had together, I could not help but let out a goofy smile. And yes, if you are following along correctly, I have tears in my eyes and am smiling like a weirdo all at the same time with chocolate glaze in between my teeth. Five hours prior, it was an impossible story for these two professional women to be engaged in a conversation about God in the setting of an old donut shop. They could have walked out a long time ago. They could have said no. They didn't have to come over to Seth's while he wore a dorky cape[4] and threw them his rickety invitation. They didn't have to agree to the random and seemingly mundane activities we entertained throughout the time spent. They could have expressed that they were uncomfortable. But the truth is, 'yes' is always a better answer when regarding God and being comfortable all of the time is a ridiculously boring life to lead.

***

I could have sounded foolish, especially in my novice Korean vocabulary. But I asked the two women before they left if we could pray for safety over their travels, their joys while on their future endeavors, and that good company may continuously surround them. To my delight, the two women looked at one another and nodded. We escorted our two new friends outside of Good Time Donuts and found ourselves standing in the middle of the vacant parking lot. The freight train was keeping a regular tempo for us all as we stood beneath the dim lighting of the shop. Nothing about this situation was probable. We found ourselves here from a

---

[4] Haircut

collection of souls deciding to say a bunch of unforced, willful, and bold 'yes'-s throughout a Friday night. It was an evening arranged by someone greater than us.

***

There are few things in life sweeter than acknowledging the fact that you let your life be open for God to use His paintbrush to connect a portion of His greater plan. It is so sweet because there is freedom in letting go of the paintbrush. You didn't do much of the work at all; you simply allowed yourself to be present in the moment. The sensation of being free of control and plunging into relentless faith in knowing He has a bigger, better plan is one that I can only parallel with freefalling. It is like an anthem with lyrics of revival and freedom. We sing it not merely with the purpose to sing, but so others can have an opportunity to listen and sing along. We sing so that others can realize their life can, too, march to the beat of a new song.

So there we stood, outside of Good Time Donuts, praying in a circle around our new friends from South Korea. The sun was rising just beyond the horizon and this was made evident by the golden tint taking over stretches of the parking lot pavement like a blanket made to fit its owner perfectly. I saw in this moment how magnificent God's plan is. *Magnificent* is a cheesy word when it is not placed accordingly, but this truly was the definition of magnificence.

He keeps painting for us a masterpiece in which He had long finished. He keeps painting for us because even though it may seem obvious for some, for others (like me) He must consistently show up so that I can be reminded that these brushstrokes in my life are interconnected with everyone else's. I am simply supposed to learn patience and understanding along the way. Maybe this is why my day-to-day circumstances seem so incomplete or unimportant. It is because I neglect to realize that I will probably never witness what greater thing is made done with them while here on earth. I forget to open my eyes to the truth that these "incomplete" and "unimportant" circumstances are truly miracles in the making, positioned by a persistent and all-knowing Father.

Here were the questions I kept wondering throughout my entire night into that morning: *How in the world did God know to keep me in South Korea just appropriately enough for me to acquire the language? Who else would have orchestrated Seth to work in a field where he interacted with South Koreans on a daily basis? Why was it that Seth and I became friends toward the latter years of our college careers so that we could still be in touch while these two businesswomen came for a visit? How is it that it all seemed to work out so perfectly that we were able to spent five hours together while the rest of the world was in slumber?*

These weren't coincidences.

These were miracles.

It was all about eternity.

It was a bigger picture than just us.

Even if my whole life was designed for just this moment so that these two women had the opportunity to hear about Jesus and what He did for us on the cross, I realized in this moment that would have been completely okay with that purpose. This life wasn't just about me. This life was about the greater plan.

***

Maybe this is kind of what heaven is like. A bunch of souls no longer wandering aimlessly, gathered and drawn near as the sun continuously rises and paints the black pavement gold. The cold ground we once stood upon all of the sudden radiates warmth and we cannot help but stand amazed. Past conversations and the stuff from yesterday just doesn't seem to matter anymore because we are too preoccupied with what is happening in the moment. And in the moment, the only thing present is Joy. I cannot explain it to you with these feeble words on paper. But what I can say is that I am not afraid to think about heaven anymore. I have experienced too many moments here on earth now to doubt that life beyond death is a real thing. I have experienced too many moments that have proven to me that real joy comes from things this world simply does not and *cannot* contain.

There has to be something more out there.

There has to be God.

There has to be heaven.

This joy I have inside me is something that a physical pain or death cannot triumph. It will prolong. And as far as hell goes, I am also sure of it. Because the rest of this truth is, this world is also broken. It reveals to us that there has to be satan. There has to be hell. This South Korean friend of mine lives in hell when her boss disrespects her or when her husband torments her with hurtful words. These are not just flakey, flimsy things. These are real circumstances and a real satan who enjoys deceiving us to believe this world is too awful for a God to be out there to care or to love. But that's the thing. There is no differentiation of good if there is no bad. The reason we need light is because darkness still exists. The reason the sun rises every morning is because we cannot live in night alone.

We have the rest of our lives to share the anthem that overflows from our hearts, the one that sings of revival and freedom. We have free passes to heaven in our possessions to give out to people while they still stand here with a choice. We have this gift, and I don't know about you, but I am dying for people to receive it. And something tells me that this desire alone is sufficient enough, that God will do the rest because He always does. He listens to my heart's cry and my murmuring of prayers. All He really asked of me was to make myself present, and I am content with knowing just that.

Until we see the day where we are able to gaze upon this masterpiece we have been so intricately placed within, I think it would do us best to walk amongst these golden pavements that won't lead us astray. It is a beautiful thing to have friends like Seth, the ones we don't have to question. The ones we trust. Period. We trust them because their intent and purpose is something beyond themselves. I do not rely on Seth simply on his own terms when I do lean on him for something; I lean on the God who holds him together, who holds me together, who holds us together and ultimately holds our world together. This is why taking a road trip in my pajamas at one in the morning is easy. This is also why I know it is a good thing to carry this anthem along to everyone I can. Because everyone deserves to know what it is like to have friends who will greet him or her in heaven one day. I hope and pray that I can spend this kind of eternity with each and every one of you.

What I am absolutely sure of is that as soon as I am done with this paragraph, I am going to walk to the gas station down the street and buy a pack of grape gummies. If they don't have any, orange or strawberry is just fine. The matter is not the point. It is in the fact that I am finished with my past and the circumstances that used to keep me captive. It is that I am moving forward with this story. Because I am confident now where I am coming from and I know where I am going when I am gone. I don't have a clue as to how long it will take or how I will get there. But it's okay, because I have God.

Chapter Eighteen:
The Next Chapter

I am not a mind reader (sometimes) but I feel like this could be a question on your mind at this point:

...So, what is the point of life?

It's not a secret, even though we often live like it is.

The point is Jesus. It was always Jesus. If you let anything else be more of the matter, you're not all wrong...but you're definitely not all right.

***

I purchased a new scarf today and it felt nice. I also received an e-mail from my friend's mom of photos from their cruise and some famous person they were with. That was pretty neat. But I was *craving* something today and in the end, really, this scarf was a waste of money to impress those who can't judge me on anything more than my good taste in attire and the cruise was but an exciting endeavor to know that they can still afford it and that their family can enjoy *something* together. Don't get me wrong, that's all fun and it's truly sweet. But I was just thinking to myself how if Jesus isn't the center of my scarf purchase, and if Jesus isn't the center of some vacation in Mexico...it really was worth nothing beyond the shadow here on earth.

I'd rather be at church. Not always literal, but in some way, shape, or form. Not necessarily the preference of others, no. But what I have learned personally throughout my twenty-one years is this: What really gives *life* into *my* life...is to not make it mine.

***

I know that most of the lessons told here are of the people I had come across or the unfolding of their lives intertwining with mine. There have been times when I used to think that I must undergo every heartache and trial myself to truly gain the insight and lesson. Before knowing God, I didn't find other's stories to be as important because they weren't my own. I didn't live them. I didn't know the experiences personally and the experiences certainly did not know me. There have also been times when I thought perhaps I shouldn't bother learning certain lessons at all in fear of pain or humiliation. But now I see it differently. I see that this was my personal struggle with letting go of my pride and my preconceived notions.

In order to truly sustain and live the good life—the only one that matters, we must welcome one another into our lives. Our stories have roles that need to be played by those we least expect. We are meant to suffer and rejoice together. Our lives are supposed to affect one another's. In fact, they already do; subtly yet wholly. We might as well make it for goodness' sake.

On the back of my annual planner, I have a sticky note that has been transferred over from one year after another. It reads:

"Learn from the mistakes of others. You can't live long enough to make them all yourself." –Eleanor Roosevelt

I think Eleanor was onto something. But I don't want to leave it at just that. Not only should we take the time to collect others' stories to learn and to engage, but we should also feel the responsibility to share what we have collected thus far. All of us. As often as possible. Not always through words, but more importantly with our actions, interactions, transactions, and transformations. If we are who we say we are and we have a great story to tell, we should not neglect to live it out. And when living out great stories, I believe we will find ourselves convinced that there's no turning back from there. The story must go on. The goodness must progress. To create room for such, we ought to cling to paragraphs like this and make sure to outline them for the times when we surely will forget. Because God knows there will be moments for the darker seasons and chapters of life. To breathe intentionally with purpose and a will for tomorrow is a rare and desirable gift. And I believe that the best thing we can do with the best things in life is to share it.

Right now in my life, the best thing is my constantly renewing relationship with Jesus. This is what keeps me breathing for tomorrow. This is what keeps my pages turning. It's no secret, nor is it something I can keep to myself. We all have stories to tell and believe it or not, God orchestrates to entangle them all together in His beautiful mastery.

Maybe the way this picture becomes clearer is by us becoming more vulnerable with one another. Maybe when we begin to tear these walls down and understand that our worlds are meant to live harmoniously, we will see that it is a story that is greater than just you and me. The roles played are not casted by our own creative minds. The lessons learned are mastered by a greater Teacher.

This story is a good one. And we are, in fact, not the main character after all. It's Jesus. It was always Jesus. Like the way these chapters and years of my small life cannot stand alone to tell something great, we are but pebbles of a remarkable monument that we have an opportunity to be a part of. In order to do this well, we ought to ask more questions to one another. We should listen more deeply. And we should care. We shouldn't talk just to talk, but to share something good. We shouldn't stay awhile because it is an obligation, but because it is our heart's honest desire.

***

Autumn is my favorite season. It reminds me that change is good, that change leads to things like colorful leaves and the opportunity to find a different coat. I'm headed to Oregon this fall to see what God is painting on the other side of this country. I anticipate spending the next year there because I'm curious and I am awake. I want to hear what the people there have to say and I have a sweet feeling that my life is supposed to be entangled with theirs.

Like seasons, we don't fully become aware of how much we appreciate the smell of home or the familiar roads of a small town until it is distant. I hope to gather more things I appreciate about this beautiful state of Michigan while I am not here. I also hope to taste different foods, try learning a new language, and maybe even surf. (I am an awful swimmer.) I hope to be broken all over again and learn that I still have so much more left to learn. Most importantly, I hope that I can share the best love story I now know about Jesus to someone new.

***

Church, to me, is no longer the prejudice, stiff, haughty brick building I attended in fear of hell. Church is the body of people who help one another, stretching from generations to races, loving with a common denominator and that being Jesus. Church, to me, is us, joining together to make it to the end, to call one another brother and sister, hoping to make this world a better reflection of heaven and its people like God Himself because we are promised it is worth it.

And because I now know that the Church is everywhere, my soul doesn't cling to a specific day, city, family, friends, or anything of this world. It doesn't even cling to my indescribably comfortable queen size bed. Because this isn't my home; this world really is a temporary place that I get a chance to impact. I can live in it as colorfully as my heart yearns and it is no longer foolish to me that I have child-like faith. My soul clings to one thing and it is Jesus.

***

I have been given the opportunity to see what this life is all about. It isn't just about me, or the fact that I messed up in the past. It isn't about my history or the people who have left me hurt. It isn't about my reputation, my possessions, my agenda, or the gaudy 401k. It's about today. It is about the truth that we have been granted yet another day, this very one right now, when it wasn't guaranteed. It is about the truth that Jesus walked here on earth years ago and it *does* matter. It is about the truth that He is the reason we live in freedom and all else is temporary.

I see the purpose now.

I see why I am here. Or there, in Oregon. Anywhere, really. It is about living in the moment and telling the story that can save lives. It is about loving with urgency and being satisfied in Him alone.

I have all I need. I have had it all along. Until the time comes when I am welcomed to rest in peace by my God himself, I'll keep turning the pages like never before. I'll keep moving forward because that is where He awaits for me.

Postscript

Hi. How was it, this book? It's my first time writing something lengthier than a ten-page research paper on dinosaur fallacies. (I told you I went to a liberal arts institution.) So, I am thankful you were willing to take this walk with me. If nothing else, I hope it encourages you to do something

I hope you push yourself off of the pavement and see that gravity doesn't have to weigh you down along with other worldly things. Or perhaps just the opposite; get off of your high horse and actually feel what it is like to hit rock bottom. Make more friends. Make fewer friends. Make different friends. Quit your horrible job. Learn what it means to let go. Or maybe you need to hold on. Find a hobby. Seek your passion. Apologize. Forgive. Pray. Pray out loud. Close the doors, shut the blinds, and admit something to yourself for the first time. Better yet, admit it to God. Hear your heart. Hear its rhythm. Listen to the clock ticking, and then escape it. Draw close to what is good and pray for those who don't get it. Allow yourself to receive undeserved gifts and find yourself giving the same. Love freely and accept truth. Stop waiting for an invitation to live your life, it's been here all along.

Acknowledgments

We could be here a while. My head is spinning with the names of every individual who probably will never know how they have played a part in shaping who I am today to have written this book. With that being said, please note that this is not in any particular order. Not that I assume we are all in third grade still with this competitive and irrationally critical concern of lists, but you never know. I would like to eternally and gratefully thank Mark and Crystal Kirgiss, Nick McKinney, Lindsay Allward, Mike and Trina Farah, Grace Theisen, Lauren Ogle, Maria Signore, and Jaron and Vicki Nyhof for their incredibly generous hands to make this project of mine possible. Tate Kirgiss for making me do this. Alex Bolen, Jared DeMeester, Lydia Wathen, Tiffany Coffing, Amy Banas, Justin Makowski, Emily Glazier, Kristen Dunn, Cara Green and JamieLee Thomas for believing in me when my ideas are never tame or completely coherent. The YoungLife community for the avenues it has provided, the lessons it has taught me, and its extraordinary gift of loving and supporting. Jazzy, the most beautiful little sister God could have blessed me with, for the late nights where you let me read to you and ask if this or that made sense...then allowed me to drag you along for the 2AM caffeine runs. Pandora, for providing me with infinite hours of classical music to steadily fuel my brain-flow and never asking for anything in return. To every door holder, life giver, feet washer, and quiet server who help us along the way, THANK YOU. And of course, the remarkable, honest, and true friends and family of mine who allowed me to write about them in my stories so that God's painting can be shared. I also want to thank *you,* for taking part in this radical life we are all engaged in. Thank you for having been present with me for the ride. Let the ultimate thanks be to God.

Application

Don't just take my word for it. Take His:

- Chapter One – *The Uncontrollables*
  - **On hardships and perseverance**
    - James 1:12, Romans 5:3-5, Galatians 6:9, 1 Peter 4:12
  - **On His consistent presence with you**
    - Psalm 37:24, 1 Corinthians 1:9

- Chapter Two – *Balloons and Hot Dogs*
  - **On our circumstances with one another**
    - Ecclesiastes 9:11, Luke 6:27-36

- Chapter Three – *Eat Your Own Soup*
  - **On comparing and gossip**
    - 2 Peter 3:17, Proverbs 6:16-19, 2 Timothy 2:23-26
  - **On arrogance**
    - 1 Samuel 2:3, Proverbs 8:13

- Chapter Four – *4x4 Relay*
  - **On endurance**
    - Hebrews 12:1-15, Hebrews 10:36

- o **On being on guard**
  - ▪ 1 Peter 5:8, Mark 13:13, Ephesians 6:13
- o **On discernment**
  - ▪ Hebrews 13:9, 1 Corinthians 16:13

- Chapter Five - Prayer Works
  - o **On believing**
    - ▪ Hebrews 11:1, 1: Peter 1:21, Philemon 1:6

- Chapter Six – *Relationship Status*
  - o **On what He did for us (the gospel)**
    - ▪ John 3:16, John 15:12

- Chapter Seven – Something About Eternity
  - o **On grieving**
    - ▪ Isaiah 41:10, Matthew 5:4, Revelation 21:4

- Chapter Eight – *Love Because*
  - o **On the definition of love**
    - ▪ 1 Corinthians 13:1-13, 1 John 4:8
  - o **On being unconditional**
    - ▪ Romans 12:9-21, Matthew 5:38-48,

- Chapter Nine – *Bob*
  - o **On being different**
    - ▪ Romans 12:2, Hebrews 10:35

- Chapter Ten – *Define Success*
  - o **On contentment**
    - ▪ Hebrews 13:5, Philippians 4:11-13
  - o **On the warnings to the rich**
    - ▪ Ecclesiastes 5:10, Matthew 6:24, 1 Timothy 6:10, Psalm 37:16-17, James 5:1-6, Revelation 3:17

- Chapter Eleven – *I'm Sorry*
  - o **On forgiveness**
    - ▪ Matthew 6:14-15, Hebrews 10:17
  - o **On humility**
    - ▪ 1 John 1:9, Acts 3:19

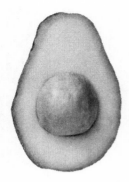

About the Avocado

- He is, in fact, a fruit. Don't call him a vegetable.
- He's actually a Superfruit. (look it up on Google.)
- He takes away the bad (LDL) in you and raises the good (HDL).
- He has thick skin. Meaning he doesn't need insurance.
- He goes with just about anything.
- He is made of nutritional content that makes your skin appear younger and brighter.
- He's good for the heart.
- He's good for babies.
- He's good for your grandpa, too.
- He's good for you.

Best part: Avocado trees do not self-pollinate. They need another avocado tree close by to bear fruit. They are a symbol of love in many cultures.

About the Author

I am flattered that you want to get to know more about me. I'm not even going to try to talk in a slyly humble third-person narrative while actually informing you on my latests and greatests in this section. (Because, to be frank, I'm uncertain what would qualify.) I am constantly changing my endeavors and locations as I utilize this sweet time of transitioning between one chapter of my life to the next. When I am not writing, I am a YoungLifer, a lifestyle photographer, and a purposeful wanderer. Currently, I am typing this on a subway and I am pretty sure I missed my stop an hour ago. Who knows, maybe we're be sitting next to each other and you haven't got a clue. Do you know where we're going? Because I sure as heck don't. You can follow my ridiculous play-by-play on Twitter: @theletterji

CPSIA information can be obtained at www.ICGtesting.com
Printed in the USA
BVOW04s2006300913

332544BV00005B/246/P